A TRUE STORY OF DETERMINATION

FIGHT TO THE END

ERIC HANNA

ISBN: 978-1-7337955-2-4

Edited by: Beth Crosby

Published by Warren Publishing
Charlotte, NC
www.warrenpublishing.net
Printed in the United States

To Owen, Cole, and Peyton.
Follow your dreams wherever they lead you.

OUR HONOR DEFEND—
WE WILL
FIGHT
TO THE
END
FOR O-HI-O STATE!

FOREWORD

The fall of 1997 was one of change for the Buckeyes and for me. Coach O'Brien was headed to Ohio State to replace Randy Ayers, who had seen the Buckeye basketball program struggle through a continual turnstile of transfers and losses during his tenure. This put me in a spot where I was going to have to either play for a new coach or head to a new school.

Coach O'Brien had a vision for me out of high school that allowed me to step into a leadership role at Boston College from day one. I grew alongside the rest of our team as we became a consistent contender within the Big East during my freshman and sophomore years. As Coach O'Brien left for the Big Ten to face a new challenge, I decided I was in for the challenge as well. After all, Coach O'Brien had always believed in me. Now it was time for me to believe in him.

As conditioning started in Columbus that September, I was in an unfamiliar role. I had to sit out a year as a red shirt transfer. Undeterred, I was focused on improving my game and being a leader. Without the chance to play in games, my leadership would have to come each day in practice. I was eager to get started. What I didn't know is that a little known walk-on named Eric Hanna was also eager to join me.

Every day after practice the real work would start and each day, Eric would be there ready to shoot, to play one on one, and most importantly, to compete. The thing that was most impressive about his interest was it was all self-driven. We had players our coaches were excited to build the future around, like Jason Singleton and Neshaun Coleman, who were upperclassmen that had shown they could help a team win. Michael Redd and Ken Johnson were promising young talents that our coaches had to develop in order to take our program to the next level. Eric was a senior afterthought. No one had really ever given Eric much of a chance to amount to anything as a player, nor had they spent any extra time trying to develop him. He was a guy that coaches mostly saw as someone who could round out a roster. This season, on the surface, looked to be no different. Eric was a holdover who would soon graduate from a program that needed change. This, however, didn't stop him from giving everything he had to make his mark before he left.

As the 1997–1998 season progressed, the team struggled to find victories, but my interest didn't wane even though I wasn't playing. I had visions of what we could do once the Schottenstein Center opened the next season. What was just as important to our team development was the effort Eric put forth. Even as the season neared its end, he continued to improve, inspiring us all to keep working toward success. Eric helped us create a foundation that would take us all the way to the Final Four that next season.

The single most important part of that foundation started with Eric being a good teammate. Above all, he is the kind of person you want next to you while you are pursuing your dreams. Enjoy the ride with Eric as your teammate while you read *Fight to the End*.

Scoonie Penn

PROLOGUE

How do you define glory? Does glory have to include riches and fame? Can glory be as simple as finding fulfillment in your love for something? For me, glory came through my basketball journey.

This book captures that experience. My story is less about record books and more about exceeding expectations, including my own. This is a story of a love affair with the game of basketball that transcended my age, level of play, and overall success. The journey isn't about leading a team in scoring but loving what you do. You will find I didn't always have this perspective, which is in large part why I wanted to write this book. My hope is that these words will help you to not lose sight of this ever-important life focus. Winning is about enjoying what you do in life.

My love for basketball brought me more joy than I ever imagined. That enjoyment was fostered in all aspects of the game and not just championships and accolades. Make no mistake, this is not an attempt to completely discount winning or achievement. You will find that during my career playing for Ohio State, I made every effort to prove I could play the game well enough to be an integral part of one of the greatest programs in the history of college basketball. In the end, love of the process is what mattered most to me.

For me, basketball was always there despite daily twists and turns. The sport became a motivator that I carried into all aspects of life. It wasn't always this way. I went through all the heartbreak and frustration most players go through. Giving up was frequently in my thoughts. Not until very late in my playing career and onward into my coaching days did I recognize how the joy of the game overcame any anguish I encountered.

The game has been amusing, humbling, ego-building, inspiring, deflating, and above all, entertainingly addictive. If I was ever sad, lonely, hurt, or lost, basketball was there for me. I always had the opportunity to grab a ball and shoot. Even if I didn't have a hoop, I could dribble. I have spent hours thinking, dreaming, and simply playing the game.

During many stages of my life, basketball has been my best friend, my therapist, my joy, and my heartache. It has taught me many life lessons including discipline, toughness, patience, teamwork, and selflessness. Basketball has meant the world to me. Even now, during times of frustration, basketball is still where I turn to ponder and reflect to help put things into perspective.

I hope that in reading this book, you are re-energized to attack whatever your passion is with a renewed fervor. If even the smallest bit of energy to persevere transfers from me to you, then writing this book was worthwhile. In the following pages, I hope you will see parallels in your own passions, triumphs, failures, and journey.

Above all, I hope my story gives you a reason to fight to the end, because what could be better in life than getting up each day and fighting for something you love?

CHAPTER 1
Quitting Before Beginning

Any journey worth taking requires a leap of faith at some point. Martin Luther King Jr. once said, "Faith is taking the first step even if you don't see the whole staircase." This is easier said than done as an adult, let alone as a kid. At nine years old, my first step into basketball was one I was initially unwilling to take.

I quit before I even started.

Lake effect snow in northeastern Ohio made winters painfully long and left this fourth grader looking for any warm place to run around. It was December, and I was heading to the Saturday morning youth basketball program at Canfield High School for the first time. I walked into the gym with anxiety that was through the roof. I looked around as if I were visiting a colony on Jupiter. Nothing felt right. I saw a handful of my classmates already there, dribbling, shooting, and engaging cheerfully. They all acted as if they were born playing the game.

I had never picked up a basketball in my life. Growing up in Canfield, a surviving "Rustbelt" community a few miles from Youngstown, we picked up baseballs and footballs, but I had never played any sport that required dribbling a ball. I immediately began to sweat in panic. I felt hopelessly unprepared. Unable to face this awkwardness, I began to speed walk directly back to my mother's car, and we promptly headed home. I never wanted to feel like that again.

A few days later, something unexpected happened. I received a phone call from a family friend named Marty Paes. He was the dad and coach of a friend who I played baseball against, and he wanted to talk to me.

Talk to me on the phone? This sounded even more awkward than the whole gym experience. Elementary school kids don't talk to adults, especially not on the phone. What in the world could he want to say to me? Does a fourth grader even have the ability to have a meaningful conversation on the phone with an adult? Was there another option? Couldn't he just mail me something?

Apparently, the mail option was not something my mother would accept, and texting wasn't invented yet, so I reluctantly took the phone. I was sweating bullets. I must have done something dreadfully wrong to have to endure a solo phone conversation with an adult. Mr. Paes frequently barked at kids when they missed ground balls in Little League, so I braced myself for the worst. I knew he was going to scold me for some sort of wrong doing. I quickly thought up an apology in an attempt to ready for the barrage of anger I was surely about to endure. I began to listen to Mr. Paes, wondering how long I would have to wait until I could say I needed to go to the bathroom or something. I'd say anything to get off the phone.

He began by saying he had seen me at the Saturday basketball program and noticed I hadn't stayed for the session. By that time, I had forgotten basketball was even a thing that people did after totally blocking out the embarrassing memory of leaving the gym without so much as taking off my coat. I thought to myself, *Great, someone actually saw me paralyzed with fear, and now they've decided to talk to me about my moment of total panic.* This phone conversation was going to be even worse than I thought!

Then Mr. Paes asked me if I would like to go back with his son John the next week. I had no idea how to say no to an adult, especially one who made kids run for days if they missed a bunt sign or a take signal! I felt as though I had no option but to say yes. After all, John was my friend. Maybe this wouldn't be the worst experience of my life. In a trance-like state, out came the word yes.

I was unaware at the time that my reluctant "yes" was the leap of faith that was needed to begin a basketball journey that would consume me. For the rest of the week, nervous energy built within me about what Saturday might hold.

GROWING INTEREST

Little things in life can add up to great big changes. In my earliest days of basketball, John Cullen, Canfield High School's varsity boys' basketball coach, did many little things to ensure our experience was special. He not only loved the game and knew it well, but he also knew that this Saturday morning program was the life blood of his future teams. He wanted to get players hooked on the game as young as possible.

Along with offering the program free of charge to all participants and throwing head bands and water bottles at us as daily prizes, Coach Cullen had the most excitable coaching staff possible, his players. We all wanted to be like them and play for the high school team. In our minds, that was the big time. They might as well have been NBA superstars. People actually paid to watch them play on Friday nights. How awesome was that?

Coach Cullen did a phenomenal job of encouraging his players to help coach us. He reminded them of the pride we should all have in the program and that they represented all the future Canfield players while they were coaching us. Therefore, they should approach the task of teaching the next generation of players with tremendous enthusiasm. That mindset was contagious. Our fourth-grade coach, Chris Calpin, personified that zeal. Chris was a sophomore at Canfield and an up and coming player in the basketball program. Finding out that Chris played on the varsity team, I begged my mother to take me to one of his games. There, I saw with my own eyes that Chris was a good player, and that convinced me to listen intently to his instruction. He had a unique way of teaching us to shoot a basketball. He said we should act like we were picking our noses and flicking it. Of course that got an overwhelmingly energetic response from a bunch of messy, nose picking, fourth-grade boys. His was a brilliant analogy.

I am not sure I can say I really followed his shooting directions perfectly (and maybe from a hygiene standpoint, that was a good thing), but I can say I was lucky enough to have the ball go through the hoop from time to time. Anyone who has ever heard the sound of the ball snapping those strings as it hits the bottom of the net knows that sound can be one of the most addicting parts of the game. Once you hear it, you will do pretty much whatever is needed to hear it again.

Being one of the taller players at the time helped me compete because I had little skill and even less understanding of what I was supposed to do. There are many memories of other players yelling at me for traveling, which was probably true on most occasions. Fortunately, this beginner had just enough height and mobility to make a good play here and there. These occasional successes inspired me to keep playing and fueled my interest to learn more.

By some stroke of luck, fate put me on a strong team. After a skills session each Saturday, we would play an average of two games, and we wound up winning a lot. In fact, we had won all of our games going into the final week. Chris pulled us together and said if we went undefeated, he would have a prize for us the next week. *A prize? What could that possibly be?* My mind raced all week with excitement, wondering if we could pull it off.

The following Saturday, we completed our undefeated season. Chris pulled us together and walked us into the varsity basketball locker room. I was on cloud nine. Getting a tour of the varsity locker room seemed like reward enough for me. We were getting the opportunity to see the place where the varsity team hung out before and after all their games. Anything beyond this would be icing on the cake.

It turned out our grand prize was nothing more than a candy bar. Seen through our youthful eyes, it felt as though he had handed out national championship rings. The award of chocolate was a small gesture, but I am not sure it could have meant any more. While the candy served as a temporary trophy, the lasting memory of our success was forever.

So was my growing love for the game.

Over the next two years, I looked forward to the Canfield Saturday basketball experience more than anything. I can still remember how much I anticipated every weekend. I frequently ran around my house shooting on a Nerf hoop while imagining I was playing at the school on Saturday morning. Sprinting through the kitchen, avoiding inanimate objects such as chairs or lamps and spinning around disinterested relatives, I envisioned attacking the hoop as if I was in another championship game. Saturday always felt too far away and winter couldn't last long enough. Cold weather ending would mean the program would be gone until next year.

It wasn't hard to get me out of bed on those Saturdays. I begged my mother for a ride as early as possible and desperately hoped I could grab a closing door behind a custodian entering the school for work. Pure joy filled me whenever I found a door unlocked or propped open. I sprinted in from the winter cold to the place where all the magic happened. Then I shot by the dim light that shined from the parking lot through a long narrow window in the doors to the gym. It wasn't much, but the narrow beam of light allowed me to see the smallest bit of the rim and the outcome of each shot. The light was faint, yet so concentrated I could see all the dust particles hovering in the air. That light made the magic possible.

Sometimes other players afflicted with the same basketball addiction also showed up early. Every once in a while, enough players came early for us to play a full court game, even though we had no lights.

Brilliant idea, right?

Slamming into another player at full speed with zero visibility became the norm. Ordinarily this kind of event might stop the game but not for these junkies. We kept playing like nothing happened. It seemed I wasn't the only one getting hooked on hoops.

At this point, I craved any chance I got to pick up a ball. It would have been an easy sell to get me to play basketball year round. If the Amateur Athletic Union (AAU) or any other travel basketball program existed in the mid 1980s, I wasn't aware, nor were my parents. My mom knew nothing about basketball. She once admitted that she didn't know the other team got the ball after a basket until I was in college. Even with her lack of hoops knowledge, she was supportive. She just wanted me to be happy. She always encouraged me but never forced any activities on me while I was growing up.

My dad and I had starkly different views of basketball. At one point, my father asked me why anyone would want to run back and forth in a gym over and over again continually grabbing a ball out of a hoop. His comment made me furious. While I was discovering the excitement of basketball, he considered it a monotonous waste of time. As I moved toward my teen years, similar comments from my father only fueled my desire to play.

THE LIGHT BULB

A light bulb is frequently used as a symbol to show someone has an idea or an "aha" moment of discovery. My basketball "light bulb" might have been turned on in that dimly lit gym in Canfield. But when I discovered the phenomenon known as March Madness, there was no doubt the switch had been flipped.

Most of America has an addiction to the madness of March, if for no other purpose than to fill out a bracket and try to predict who will be crowned national champion. My first encounter with this intoxicating phenomenon was during a magical run in the 1985 NCAA basketball tournament. The championship game pitted the upstart, eighth-seeded Villanova Wildcats against the overwhelmingly favored number-one-seed, Georgetown Hoyas. It was set up to be a David versus Goliath match up.

Playing the part of David would be Villanova, which had lost ten games during the regular season, twice to the Hoyas.

I can't imagine anyone picked them to win other than family and friends (probably close family and very close friends). The Hoyas, playing the role of Goliath, had five future NBA players, featuring 7'0" center, Patrick Ewing, the eventual number one overall pick in the NBA draft and the most giant human being I had ever seen in my nine years. Georgetown had clobbered number-three-ranked St. John's in the semi-final game, so beating Villanova appeared to be a mere formality to be swept aside before the Hoyas hoisted the trophy as back-to-back NCAA champions.

In David versus Goliath, who isn't rooting for David?

Lying on our living room floor, I watched every play of a televised basketball game for the first time. I hung on to every single possession intently, as if I had been a Villanova fan since the school began their basketball program. Each possession seemed like an eternity, in part because in basketball terms, it was. This was the last year that the NCAA played without a shot clock, so each team could hold onto the ball as long as it wanted. The Wildcats took only twenty-eight shots in the entire game. (Forty-eight shots was the lowest per game average in college basketball during the 2017–2018 season.) Even with the slow pace, the game seemed to hang in the balance with every pass.

Villanova's coach, Rollie Massimino, paced the sidelines, sweating profusely, yet charismatically encouraging his team through every twist and turn. As the second half ticked away, Coach Massimino got more and more disheveled in appearance. The Wildcats stood strong, hanging on to a slim lead with the basketball world watching. Late in the game, Georgetown had knocked the ball out of bounds after a basket to stop the clock. With only two seconds remaining, Villanova had a two-point lead and the ball. The Wildcats only needed to pass the ball inbounds without a turnover to win. Even this was nerve-racking as Dwayne McClain, a Villanova guard, fell to the ground after getting tangled up with a Georgetown defender. The passer realized he had tripped and showed tremendous savvy, throwing the ball low enough that it found its way to McClain's arms. He cradled the ball while lying on the court as time expired. Villanova's title win was one of the most improbable victories in NCAA championship history.

Villanova had to play the perfect game that night to win, and by all accounts they did. They shot 78.6 percent from the floor. No one ever could have imagined they'd shoot that percentage for a half, let alone the entire contest. The Hoyas had to want a rematch. Sorry Georgetown, college basketball gives only one chance. This kind of upset has become the phenomenon that college basketball fans have come to expect to see every March. Any fan that watched Villanova win had to believe that basketball was a game of miracles, and anyone who put their mind to it could do something special. Anxiously, I began to count the days until our winter basketball program would begin again.

EARNING IT

If March Madness was the light bulb that turned on my love for basketball, that bulb only got brighter when I was introduced to the NBA. The first player I became obsessed with was Earvin "Magic" Johnson of the Los Angeles Lakers. In June 1985, the Lakers finally beat the Boston Celtics in the NBA finals for their first-ever head-to-head title. From then on, I was awestruck by his talent, and I wanted a piece of the excitement, or at least the merchandise.

I dragged my mother to Foot Locker with the goal of getting new basketball shoes for the upcoming season. Even with lots of shoe options to consider, I was already sold that I wanted Magic's shoe. *Converse* included this shoe in the *Converse Weapons* series, headlined by Magic, Larry Bird, Mark Aguirre, and Bernard King. At that time, the *Converse Weapon* was one of the premier basketball shoes being made. The price tag for a pair of these babies was a whopping sixty-three dollars. In today's shoe market that would be a steal. In 1980s terms, it was a small fortune and more money than this kid had ever seen at one time.

Normally, I would have been embarrassed to ask my mother for that kind of money. She consistently penny pinched to help us get by while living in a modest section of our overall affluent community. I must have really wanted those shoes, because I asked anyway. I waited for her to let me down easy, as I knew that the shoes were a pipe dream the moment the request left my lips. Then my mother made the best parenting move anyone could make.

My mom didn't say yes, but she said I could earn the money myself to buy the shoes. I was fine with working for it, as I desperately wanted to fit in with the "well-to-do" kids in our community. To earn sixty-three dollars would take some time. I remember mowing plenty of lawns and completing a variety of odd jobs. One that stuck out in my mind was painting our back porch. It took what seemed like an eternity, and upon completion, I'm sure it looked hideous. Nonetheless, my work eventually paid off, and we headed back to the mall for those shoes.

Standing in Foot Locker with money in hand, I prepared myself to buy those shoes I had been so certain would make me play like Magic Johnson. For a moment though, all my labor made me think long and hard about the purchase. My mother had instilled in me the value of a dollar, and I had to make sure this was what I truly wanted. After a few minutes of deliberation, I went through with the purchase. I wanted those shoes to last forever, so I made the calculated decision to buy them about a size too big. I proceeded to wear them until they hurt my feet, which was the basketball equivalent of almost two full seasons. While they were durable, they also weighed what seemed like forty pounds. They were easily the heaviest basketball shoes I have ever worn. I didn't move fast before I got the shoes. After, it frequently seemed as if I were anchored to something on the court.

Of course, since I had to have the style endorsed by Magic Johnson, the shoes were Lakers' colors. The bright purple and yellow didn't go so well with our school colors of red and black. In fact, they couldn't have clashed any more if I tried. Still, that pair of shoes was everything I wanted and more. I had to look ridiculous, but when I wore them, I was Magic Johnson, dreaming of stardom in high-tops.

Heavy, bulky, gaudy leather high-tops.

Stardom, however, was the furthest thing from where I was. I hung on to make the sixth-grade travel team after a more than shaky tryout performance. I was beyond nervous, and butterflies fluttered in my stomach throughout the experience. As the old saying goes, it is okay to have butterflies, the key is getting them to fly in formation. In my early days of basketball, my butterflies did anything but fly in formation.

Having barely made the team, I relished the opportunity to practice every day after school in our middle school gym as we prepared for tournaments. I felt special walking through the halls after school on the way to practice. Time in the gym felt like a gift. The practices felt like an elite version of the Saturday morning program with a super team of players. Once we played real games, in real uniforms against teams with players from other nearby schools, this could only get better, right?

Wrong.

I rarely saw the court during games and for good reason. I was clueless about the whole game experience. Certainly I was a novice when it came to understanding a game where the rule book was strictly followed by real officials, but I had no idea how oblivious I was. This was never more apparent than when one of my shots actually went in for the first and only time. That's right, I made exactly one basket during the sixth-grade travel season.

One basket.

My one and only hoop came in a 30–2 blowout when I made a short jump shot in the lane during the final moments, long after the outcome of the game had been decided. After the ball went in, I circled out and around the edge of the court running past our bench instead of heading back on defense. I looked at every player as I ran by, thinking they were all going to get up and give me a pat on the back or a high five. They didn't. It was like yelling and screaming, thinking that you won the lottery, only to find you read the numbers wrong. They all looked at me like I had three heads, wondering why I was so elated with such a routine act. I am sure our coaches also thought this kid taking his own individual victory lap around the gymnasium was half-crazy as well.

Looking back, that moment summed up how completely naïve I was about the grand scheme of basketball. One can only imagine how much of a fish out of water I was beyond this one memorable incident. Still, for one small moment, scoring a basket gave me hope that maybe I could grow my game to something bigger in the future.

CHAPTER 2
Learning the game

Trying out for the seventh-grade team the next year meant a whole season of enjoyment and the first step to being part of the Canfield Cardinals basketball program for years to come, at least I hoped. Our tryout yielded a roster of eighteen players. It seemed like an absurd amount for a basketball team. Nonetheless, I had a uniform, and I couldn't wait to wear it.

My seventh-grade coach, Loren Mitchell, is someone our community admired for his enthusiasm and discipline. His delivery was always passionate as he taught the game. He spoke to us about the rules and how we should play down to the smallest details. Our halftime speeches were in a nearby classroom. Spit and chalk flew as he passionately gave tips, like to "chin the ball" on rebounds to protect it. The basics he taught us would help my game for years to come.

During my seventh-grade season, we played in a dinky, archaic cafeteria gym. If someone didn't run a broom around the floor prior to practice, it would play more like an ice rink, thanks to the food scraps and trash that remained from lunch. The gym had an ancient scoreboard that could have been used in the movie *Hoosiers*. For some reason, the clock showed fourths of seconds, and to this day, I still don't know how we read it. Before every game, visiting coaches spent ten minutes trying to explain to their players how to decipher how much time was left while playing. The coaches' explanations never worked. Every single game, without fail, a player on either team would randomly chuck up a shot from long distance in the middle of the quarter thinking time was about to run out, when at least two or three minutes remained. That old clock made for an adventure every time we played a home game.

Our cafeteria gym was so short that it had an extra over and back line that was used on either side of half court so you had enough room to play. It was so narrow there was no room for three-point lines in the corners. I'm sure it wasn't as noticeable prior to my seventh-grade season because there were no three-point lines in Ohio high school basketball. Now that the line was part of the game, the constricted court glared with insufficiency. All the extra and missing lines made the gym look like a *Pac Man* game gone bad. Nevertheless, we had our own gym as seventh graders, which was pretty cool in my book.

Coach Mitchell was excited about the thought of the new three-point shot and he got us all revved up to make the first one in school history. He schemed constantly to come up with plays that would give us a good opportunity to score that first shot. The chance finally came in a home game against arch-rival Poland Middle School.

On one of the first few possessions of the game, much to the displeasure of Coach Mitchell, a player from Poland beat us to the honor. The player, who can only be described as rotund in stature, caught the ball at the top of the key and nailed the shot. The look on Coach Mitchell's face is still etched in my mind. He looked as if someone had just deflated the tires of his car and keyed the driver side door for good measure. The whole team reacted as if someone closed the circus right before we walked in. We got trounced the rest of the game, paving the way to a very mediocre season.

LIFE LESSONS

We didn't win a lot that season, but I did gain some valuable lessons. One came when we played on the road at the quaint little neighboring town of Salem. Our team walked into the tiny little bandbox of a gym that had an overhead running track so close to the court, you couldn't shoot from the corners without hitting it. We were all dressed up in sweaters and ties, trying to mentally prepare for the game. While in the visitor's locker room getting ready for the game, a feeling of horror came over me. My mother had packed my white home uniform for the game instead of our away red jersey. I started to panic, but I knew that Salem was a quick ten-minute drive from my house, so my mom could easily bring my road uniform to the gym so I could still play in the game. I hurried over to tell Coach Mitchell my predicament so I could try to resolve the situation as quickly as possible and get back to the normal pregame routine.

When I told Coach Mitchell, he had a different plan for how to resolve the problem. He told me not to call my mom. He said I was too old to be relying on my mother to pack the correct uniform, and it was my responsibility to bring what I needed for each game. As a result, my consequence would be that I would sit on the bench in my dress clothes and cheer for the team. I would not be in uniform that night.

I was devastated. I remember the miserable feeling of sitting on the sidelines as the team went through warm-ups and as the game began. With no uniform on, I had no shot of playing. It wasn't as if I played much anyway, but having no chance to play was really disheartening. I also felt like I let Coach Mitchell down. I cheered like crazy that night in an effort to compensate for my irresponsible misstep.

The valuable lesson that night was to take ownership for myself. I was the one who couldn't play without a uniform, so I needed to take responsibility for it. Throughout the rest of my basketball career, I always checked my bag to make sure I had all my uniforms, shoes, and everything I needed for the game. I wouldn't let an equipment issue keep me out ever again.

As the season neared its end, Coach Mitchell pulled me aside along with one other player, my friend John Paes. Neither of us had started a game during the season. He explained that he was going to start one of us in the last game based on our efforts throughout the season. He was going to choose one of us after the practices leading up to the game. That meant we each had about a week to impress him enough to earn the spot.

This was energizing news! Starting meant you were a good player, right? Who doesn't want to do that? It was time to prove my worth in practice. It was time to dive for loose balls, hustle back a little harder on defense, and put my body in harm's way to make a play. After a week of practice, when that last regular season game came, John was in the starting line-up. Being happy for a friend in this moment is a real ask of empathy for a developing seventh grader when your hopes have been dashed at the same time. Still, the fact Coach Mitchell considered starting me gave me hope for my basketball future.

Coach Mitchell worked hard to keep eighteen players in the mix, but that wasn't easy. I didn't help myself with the uniform mishap and illnesses over the winter. On the whole,

I saw the court sparingly, and I scored a single basket for the second year in a row.

One basket—the entire season—again.

We closed out our season with a 5–6 record. Once more, I was going to need to get better, or this could be a short-lived career.

AWKWARD AGE

Eighth grade is a constant battle of hormones, immaturity, awkwardness, and embarrassment for virtually everyone. Throw in some facial acne and a voice crack here or there, and I was as miserable as the next kid. I stopped hanging out with many of my childhood friends who lived in the neighborhood. They had all lost interest in sports or did immature things while they hung out, mostly out of boredom. My father came home from work each night around nine o'clock or so, which meant we didn't do anything together or bond. I know my dad loved me, but knowing he didn't appreciate my love for the game made building a relationship hard. It was hard not to be jealous of the kids whose dads played outside with them or those who had older brothers to play one-on-one. I had a sister who was glued to our piano. All of this added up to many hours of shooting and dribbling (or at least attempting to) alone on our gravel driveway. Basketball season couldn't come soon enough.

My eighth-grade season came with a few less players making the team, fifteen in total, but much more winning. Tony Ross, our eighth-grade coach, was ultra-competitive and encouraged us to find our winning spirit. Unfortunately, this came at the expense of even less personal playing time. Less game opportunity added to my desperation to get better and be a part of the action.

Who doesn't love winning?

When our star point guard hit a half-court shot to win a game against neighboring Boardman Middle School, we were all excited. Still, I hadn't even taken my warm-ups off, and I couldn't help but feel somewhat dejected. Since I hadn't played, I felt like it really didn't matter if I was there. It felt like everyone was cheering around me, not with me. It was a selfish, yet natural response that many teens experience and struggle to make sense of at this stage, especially if they are devoid of a voice of reason.

My basketball frustrations carried over to everyday eighth-grade life as well. Frequently at recess, we headed for the outdoor courts to play basketball. The games were typical of middle school recess with too many players and not enough basketballs. Everyone wanted to be the point guard so they could have all eyes on them. Consistent taunting abounded with foul language that eighth graders think validates their maturity when out of their teachers' ear shot.

Things got extra hard for me when we lined up to head inside. Daily, I faced the ridicule of one individual who wanted me to hear how bad he thought I was. He shouted things like, "I can't believe you are on the basketball team," and "Why do you even play? You are horrible." He got inches from my face as if he wanted me to shove him to start a fight. I tried to ignore him, but it happened repeatedly and continually bothered me. However, I wanted to play basketball and fit in so badly, I just lived with the harassment. Constant bullying like this made me hate recess and middle school in general.

So, like any other self-conscious early teen, I spent all my time trying to blend in and hang on for dear life to the few things that inspired me. Whether it was a Michael Jordan dunk or tales of Abraham Lincoln told by Mr. Reel in American history class, I had to find something to keep me going.

The team kept winning, and I kept sitting. I was struggling to feel like I mattered on our much-improved team. I was searching for a glimmer of basketball hope and found it when Coach Ross added an assistant coach to help us out. Chris Calpin, my fourth-grade coach, was home from college for winter break. His coaching stint was just long enough to help me get back on track. He helped inspire me to fight on throughout the rest of eighth grade, even when my role seemed to be almost nonexistent.

Coach Calpin kept me going with a fresh perspective of our team. Coach Ross showed us how successful we could be down the road. We finished 14–2 with dreams of stardom in high school ahead.

I again scored my one basket … for the season.

As for my basketball future, it was like listening to a broken record (or a retweet for those who didn't live in the era of records). The need for improvement was an understatement and a necessity if I was to join in for what was seemingly turning into a fun ride.

GYM RAT

Even though I played sparingly that eighth-grade season, I couldn't get enough basketball. I was ready to play whenever and wherever I could. All other interests had gone by the wayside. It was all basketball now. Living about a block and a half from Canfield Middle School, I would head over to the outdoor courts by myself to work on my game. If there was snow, I took a shovel with me to make space to dribble and shoot. I wore gloves, eventually shedding them as my fingers and extremities warmed up. I was desperate to improve upon my current average of one basket … per year.

Desperate to find a warmer, flatter, and less windy option for working on my game, I decided to take a new approach. I had to find a way inside to shoot after the school day ended. I started propping open one of the doors near the cafeteria gym as I left school, and I would come back after the custodians had cleaned that area to get some shots up.

Being in the gym to shoot was heaven, except when I wasn't permitted to be there. Talk about nerve-racking! With every shot I took, I wondered if someone was coming and what my escape route was. Knowing I wasn't supposed to be in the gym, I often ran when I heard any noises that sounded like a custodian. The final straw was hearing footsteps, then what sounded like running, then definitely some yelling as I sprinted out the side door. I didn't stop running until my feet hit our back porch.

I've always subscribed to the idea that doing the right things makes it easy to sleep at night. Sneaking in the gym and sprinting out at the first sign of life was not helping me sleep, so I scrapped sneaking back in until I could come up with a better plan. Until then, I would have to adapt to the unpredictable weather that makes Ohio such a colorful place. As many Ohioans say, if you don't like the weather, wait five minutes, and it will change. Layered clothing became the most important preparation besides bringing a basketball.

For the rest of the off-season, it was me, a ball, and a hoop. I cherished that time then and now. Any opportunity to get some shots up is a little slice of heaven. Whether I was sad, disappointed, or frustrated as all teenagers are, that was my outlet. I spent many uncomfortable days shooting. It helped me cope with bullies and think about how to talk to girls, among other teen crises. Shooting hoops helped me work through the changes during this awkward life stretch.

CHAPTER 3

High school low

As the summer before entering high school progressed, my physical growth did not. I headed into high school looking like a seventh grader.

A weak seventh grader.

My weight was about 125 pounds to be generous, and strength can often beat skill in basketball. If basketball was a windshield, I was consistently a bug. Once described by Coach Mitchell as needing to "run around in the shower to get wet," I knew a lack of girth was jeopardizing my chance to compete. Not only did the hits hurt, they sapped my energy to the point that I couldn't keep up with the more physically mature players. Even with a couple of star players moving up to the junior varsity team as freshmen, there were still plenty of players ahead of me. My now 5'8" frame kept me on the perimeter as an average size guard with slow feet. This is a deadly combination and not in a good way. I managed to make the team that season, but the minutes I salvaged came when the visiting team was warming up the buses.

As a sophomore, I was a towering 5'9½", making me the second shortest player in our program. I wore size thirteen shoes, but that served only to make me more awkward. I was a slow, left-handed point guard with big feet who was built like an Erector Set. Some of our coaches took to calling me the "praying mantis," which I wasn't really sure how to take. My arms and legs were headed in every direction except where they were supposed to go. I was lucky to even be on the team based on my lack of fluidity. Practicing daily against mature juniors and seniors was a constant reminder of how far I was from impacting our program.

Seeing the court during games sophomore season became even more of a mirage than ever before. For the first time, I was consistently the last player to get my number called. On several occasions, I was the only player who didn't get in. I felt insignificant and inferior. Some of the older players physically and verbally made playing miserable, and a couple freshman players were getting minutes ahead of me. I craved belonging but found few moments that told me I fit in.

Still, I never regretted the decision to play that season. I cherished being a part of a team. Even if I didn't connect socially with many of the other players, we all shared in the joy we gained from basketball. The opportunity to learn about the game was motivation enough for me to be there. I took pride in wearing a Canfield Basketball jacket. Our program was well respected, so just being involved kept me going. I continued hoping that something would happen to help me expand my role in the program.

After practice one day near the end of my sophomore year, I was standing in the hall looking at the trophy cases while waiting for a ride home from my mom. A doctor had stopped by to give an update on an injured player and paused for a moment and stood next to me. The doctor began to size me up. He looked me up and down and then asked me a peculiar question: "Where does your hip stop?"

I though this was a relatively uncomfortable way to start a conversation, and I still wasn't thrilled at age fifteen about making small talk with adults, especially ones who started a conversation in this fashion. Nervously, I pointed to the top of my hip. He responded with a somewhat unexpected level of excitement and stated that he felt I was going to end up being very tall. I faked an awkward laugh, hoping that would end our exchange because the sooner it was over, the better. I went back to staring at trophies and plaques.

Really tall. Yeah right.

I didn't put much stock into his statement because I was born to parents who were 5'8" and 5'11". I could have guessed that maybe I'd grow three more inches or so but not much more. I guess he knew something I didn't.

WALKING AWAY

The Canfield basketball program was headed in the right direction after winning four straight Mahoning Valley Conference titles; however, it was not because of me. I still treasured being on the team but wondered if there was even a place on the team for me anymore. As an undersized junior, every fiber of my being had me thinking I wouldn't earn a spot on the roster that season. I had never been cut from a team, and I was terrified at the thought of it happening to me now. With this in mind, I decided not to try out my junior year. That's right, I didn't even try out. The kid who ate, slept, and breathed basketball was too afraid of getting cut to try out.

I walked away.

What was the main reason I didn't try out? I did not want to hear, "You aren't good enough." I think this is a natural concern for many young players today but also one that needs to be dispelled. What I didn't realize at the time was that not knowing how well I played was much worse than getting cut. So many of us who make a choice like this wind up playing the "what if" game. If I had tried out and possibly played my junior year, if I had been on the team and played sparingly, who knows what relationships might have formed and how much better I would have become. This is all aside from the fact that I was still desperate to play the game and would have found joy in practicing each day, regardless of friendships or accomplishments.

If you find something you have a true passion for, don't let it go when you still have the opportunity to enjoy it. If the object of your affection rejects you, well then, at least you know you gave what you had in your heart.

Instead, I got a job after school at a local sports card and apparel store thinking this would surely fill my need for an athletics fix. My job was to work behind the counter and help customers with shirts, hats, baseball cards, and collectibles. All the while, I talked sports with customers. I left school every day and drove straight to work, clocking in about three o'clock and closing the store about nine o'clock, eventually heading home and finally nodding off while trying to finish trigonometry homework. It started all over again the next day and continued on during most weekends.

We always had a TV on behind the counter so customers could follow what was going on in the sports world. One day that fall, Magic Johnson came on with a special report and told everyone he had contracted the Human Immunodeficiency Virus (HIV) and was retiring. Everyone in the store was floored by the news, and we discussed it for weeks. I was sad to hear that my first basketball hero was done playing. As the year moved on, we talked about whatever the sports topic of the day was while trading cards and selling hats and shirts. Getting paid to talk sports was a dream scenario, right? What could possibly be better? Well, there was one thing that could be better.

Playing.

Late in my junior year, our high school had a spirit week that culminated in a home game and dance on Friday night. As usual, I couldn't attend the game because of work, but the dance was after the varsity game, so I could make it. I very much needed this break from my non-stop schedule to hang out with my peers.

As planned, I got there after the game was over. I walked through the gym and headed toward the cafeteria where the dance was to be held. The game had ended about a half an hour before, so the lights in the gym were still dimmed over the bleachers leaving a theatrical presence hovering over the court. Kernels of popcorn were strewn about, and the distinct gym smell lingered. That undeniable scent of hardwood mixed with a hint of basketball leather was forever etched in my memory from my early days of basketball. The aroma quickly triggered a sense of happiness that I had never found off of the court. It evoked childhood memories of finding a way in the gym every Saturday morning in hopes of shooting a few extra shots on the varsity court. This unexpected euphoria was so distinct I couldn't ignore it. It was a warm sensation of pure joy that I found only while playing basketball. It evoked feelings I hadn't felt in a long, long time.

That two-minute walk across the gym abruptly changed my fate. I was convinced I had made a mistake not trying out that season. I could not find the sensation I felt walking through the gym anywhere else, and I had to try to get that back. I had to give it another shot. I knew there was a good chance I would end up getting cut, but after my trip down memory lane, that didn't matter. To have another shot at playing was worth anything. I decided I would devote all my free time between that moment and tryouts the next fall to regaining that feeling.

LIKE MIKE

Every player who has ever picked up a basketball in the Midwest experiences a transformation that occurs early in March. About the time the March Madness brackets come out, the weather begins to improve. This combination drives every basketball addict to do two things: first, to turn on the NCAA tournament to watch the magic and second, to head out into their driveways and onto neighborhood courts to try and emulate that magic.

It can't be helped. March Madness is a rite of passage. By spring, anybody and everybody is ready to get outside and move around without snow. The weather always feels a little colder than you want and a little windier than you hoped for, but this tradition makes February feel like a thing of the past. Even if we still have to shovel away the melting remains of winter, nothing can stop this time-honored tradition. Couple the weather with NCAA tournament fun, and a sort of basketball "cabin fever" epidemic hits. The madness that particular season was Christian Laettner's shot to beat Kentucky in the regional finals in overtime. Many still consider that shot to be the greatest not only in tournament history, but basketball history as well. Whether you loved or hated Duke, you had to get out on the driveway to attempt to recreate that buzzer-beating moment for yourself.

With my recent rededication to the game I missed so much, I couldn't wait to get outside and get to work. A quick drive over to the high school let me play for the first time since school began the previous fall. The school had just installed two beautiful new outdoor courts, and I wanted to try them out. As I began to shoot, the ball caromed off into the melting snow piles. I ran it down, wiped it off, and began again. It felt great to be playing again after such a long time away from the game.

I took some casual jump shots as most players do when warming up. After I had loosened up a bit, I began to play at more of a game-like speed. I started to dribble toward the basket, slashing in as if I were Michael Jordan knifing through the Pistons' physical defense. I went up to lay the ball in over the front of the rim. As I jumped, I quickly realized things were drastically different from when I had played more than a season ago.

Since my sophomore season, I had experienced a summer of waking up in the middle of the night with terrible shin pain. Every time I looked down, it seemed, my jeans were too short. I think we went shopping for new pants at least three times the following year. Heck, I even received two after-school detentions for wearing shorts that didn't cover enough of my legs. What I hadn't noticed was my current height. I had grown to about 6'4" and was still waking up in pain nightly. Because of my absence from the court, I hadn't noticed the entirety of my transformation.

When I went up to lay the ball in, I realized how much higher I rose than before. Instead of rolling the ball off my fingertips, I dunked it.

I dunked the basketball!

What had just happened? It was like the movie *Like Mike* without the Michael Jordan sneakers and the lightning strike that make the main character's basketball shoes turn him into a sort of basketball super hero. I suddenly felt the impact of growing six-and-a-half inches in one year! Like anyone would in this moment, I had to see if I could do it again!

For most players, dunking is a multi-step, multi-year process. It starts in middle school when players attempt to touch the net and then the backboard. The next step (or leap) of dunking moves to grabbing the basket goal, which is usually followed by a PE teacher yelling, "Stay off the rims!" Finally, if a player is lucky enough to get so far, he goes through the "What can I dunk?" stage. Most begin with golf balls and tennis balls, eventually moving to volleyballs and then the real thing. The last time I drove to the hoop, I could barely touch the backboard, but that was many months—and many inches—ago. I skipped most of the progression and went straight for the good stuff. Talk about a game changer! If I wasn't sold on playing before, I definitely had a new reason to give it another shot!

As much as I'd like to go on to tell you how this turned me into an all-league player overnight, I had no such luck. To put it in perspective, playing basketball at this height was like giving the keys of an eighteen-wheeler to a sixteen-year-old who just got his learner's permit. Sure, the kid would have some understanding of how to drive a car, but a semi-truck? Good luck with that! I had absolutely no idea how to use my new basketball body. I had left the game my sophomore year as a small, slow guard. In the '90s almost no tall players played away from the basket. Now I was going to be a post player. This meant I'd have to play inside with my back to the basket against big, strong, imposing players. To say I was clueless and awkward in my new body and in this new position would be putting things nicely.

I spent the whole summer on those outdoor courts behind the high school trying to refine my game. Looking back, I should have asked my high school coaches about getting involved, but I was thinking their reaction might make me lose hope before tryouts even happened. So, I didn't really say much until fall conditioning. I practiced and played on my own. If there was anyone there to play against, I joined in. If not, I practiced and dreamed of a second chance.

PROVE AND IMPROVE

At tryouts that fall, the coaching staff created a list of people Coach Cullen needed to "talk to." I was so nervous. I had never been cut from a team before. Would this be it? Waiting in the varsity locker room while looking into the coaches' office through a large glass window was about as nerve-racking as anything imaginable. Another senior who had played every season since seventh grade was in there talking to the entire staff. He was a marginally talented point guard competing with an up-and-coming sophomore who needed game minutes to grow. I found out later he was told he could be on the team, with no guarantee of playing time. He chose to walk away.

My turn came next. As I sat in nervous anticipation, Coach Cullen told me I was not getting cut, but I shouldn't expect to play when games started. He went on to say our core group of post players was chock full of talent and experience, so I would fight an uphill battle to ever see the court in games. This wasn't a tough decision. I chose to stay. In fact, I was good to go when I heard the words, "You're not getting cut."

I couldn't wait to get started. I was part of the team again. Sure, I would have liked to have more assurance that I would play, and I would struggle early on when even the sophomores played in front of me, but I enjoyed being part of the team so much that sitting on the bench was still worth it. Honestly, I really never fully believed I could make the varsity team, so this was all a bonus. I was optimistic about having a great year because I was doing what made me happiest.

I was playing basketball again.

As expected, the first time our team took the floor that season, I remained on the bench because of the talent in front of me. To give an indication of how good they all were, we out-rebounded our opponents by 11.2 rebounds per game that season. Those individuals needed to be on the floor. That left me with a void of playing time in games, but I was improving each day in practice. After my year away from the game, any opportunity to play helped me improve.

Most teams have a fan favorite who doesn't actually get to play much. For some reason, whether I just played hard or I looked like a wind puppet while I was on the court, fans supported me. Maybe it was because of the showy dunks I would attempt during warm-ups. Our student announcer even gave me the nickname "the Eighth Wonder of the World" because my height and length gave me a unique physical appearance. I weighed about 165 pounds at the time and would be best described as a toothpick in high tops. Frequently during games, the crowd would chant "E – H, E – H, E – H!" in an effort to force our coach's hand into playing me more.

I appreciated their support. Even if I wasn't playing much, the fans seem to enjoy my presence. Whether it was the chants or the signs with my nickname that friends hung up all over the school, I felt more valued than I had in years. Slowly, I began to improve, and I started seeing a few minutes in games, even when the game was still in doubt.

TRUE CARDINAL

Before I could blink, Senior Night was upon us, and we were playing Youngstown East High School. Of the five seniors on the team, four normally started with one sophomore. Then Coach Cullen brought in a couple juniors and four more sophomores off the bench, along with yours truly, for a few sporadic moments. As basketball tradition goes, coaches often start all their seniors on Senior Night as a reward for their efforts. Personally, I wanted to play when it would help the team win. When Coach Cullen kept our regular starting lineup against East, I was fine with his decision. Whatever he thought would help us win was okay by me. So, I was the only senior who didn't start, but that didn't mean I couldn't contribute to a win.

Early in the first half, I was given my first chance to take the floor. My game had improved throughout the season, and I had become more assertive with my play. As our lead mounted, I continued playing aggressively. I finished up leading the team in scoring with fifteen points in a lopsided victory. To have such a big role in our senior night win was especially rewarding. It was also gratifying to think I was playing my best basketball as I neared the end of my senior season.

We concluded the regular season with a record of 14–6. While six losses were unheard of at that time in Canfield, we managed another league title, sharing the crown with Girard. We both had won against the other at home during the regular season, and we met again in the district tournament. After a gut-wrenching performance, we lost in double overtime 70–69. We all had a hollow feeling inside like our time had run out too soon. We all were left wondering, "What if?"

Remembering a turnover I had in the game that ended in a three-point play at the other end left me wishing there was a way to turn back time.

The end of any sports season is abrupt. One day you are playing for championship glory and preparing several hours every day to achieve that glory. During the other hours of the day, you are completely consumed with the chase for that glory. Then bang! It all stops. You feel a void that is almost as if there were a death in the family. Everything you have worked for so tirelessly has just ended. You cannot prepare for the abrupt nature or the finality. The team that you sacrificed for, that you went through all the highs and lows with and the family bond that had been created was now a thing of the past. The loss cut even deeper when I considered this was my last competitive season. I felt as if I was no longer a basketball player. I didn't like the feeling, but I had to cope with it. No colleges even knew who I was or fathomed the idea of recruiting me.

Our basketball banquet soon followed and brought closure to our season. We celebrated our league title. In the backs of our minds, however, we knew that our archrivals Girard and Campbell Memorial, the fourth-place team in our conference, both were still playing and chasing state tournament glory. That was salt in the wounds of our "what could have been" dreams. We had lost to both of those teams in close games in their gyms and then dismantled them when they played in ours. I couldn't help but think about the possibilities. Our team had a lot to be proud of, but I think we all had a vacant feeling that we had left some opportunities on the table.

I was named Most Improved Player in our program, sharing the award with Anthony Garono, another senior who was an all-league player that season. Anthony was a huge part of our success, so sharing the award with him made me believe I had definitely made tremendous strides.

Considering I wasn't even in the program the year before, I felt even more affirmed. As Coach Cullen wrote in a letter to our team that was included in our banquet program, "We will not soon forget Eric's metamorphosis from a skinny sophomore who only dreamed of playing, to a true Cardinal." His statement meant a lot to me. I was a valued member of a highly respected basketball program.

Coach Cullen surprised me when he spoke about the seniors and gave us each our varsity letters. When he spoke of me, he said, "Eric is going to be a heck of a player when he's twenty." At the time, I thought that was a really nice compliment, but I had played only seventy-one minutes the entire season.

That's right, a total of seventy-one minutes.

That is the equivalent of fewer than three games, or a little over three minutes per game. How would this translate into great play two years from now? Where would I be playing when I was twenty? The answer, I assumed, was nowhere. No one was recruiting me. No one saw me play but a few minutes at a time. If I was to be really good at age twenty, it appeared I would be in a church league somewhere. At least that was my opinion. I guess Coach Cullen was more of a basketball visionary than I was.

The basketball season wasn't yet over for Girard and Campbell, both of which went on to win state in Divisions II and III. A close friend, Chris Thomas, and I had made a deal that we would go to the state basketball tournament no matter what. From the seats we purchased in their student sections, we agonizingly watched both teams cut down the nets. The tournament produced two state champions from our conference, and we had tied for the league title. With our team being so close, and my role gradually growing, I couldn't help but leave this experience wishing for a chance for more basketball in my future. I felt so close to a dream, but I also felt like I didn't have a path to reach it.

Our trip to Columbus had another purpose besides watching basketball. Both Chris and I had decided to attend The Ohio State University and room together. When we went down to OSU, we were excited to look around and see our future home. We explored the campus and got our fill of the state tournament. We even did a little souvenir shopping, buying some gear that we could wear around Canfield to let everyone know we were going to be Buckeyes in the fall. We headed home with some optimism and some apparel after getting our initial taste of what was to come in Columbus.

CHAPTER 4
Higher Education

I started my college experience in the fall of 1993 at The Ohio State University like many other freshmen: energized and clueless. My initial focus was gaining solid academic footing. By the spring quarter, my GPA was high enough to enter the Fisher College of Business. I got involved on campus and made some extra money by officiating volleyball within the intramural program. I enjoyed every minute of living hours away from home, on my own, and in a totally new environment. Other than my high school friend Chris, I held onto only one link from the past. I still loved to play basketball.

I showed up at Larkins Hall, the main recreational facility, to play basketball at least four or five days every week. Two courts in the red gym were always available for pick-up basketball games late into the afternoon. The real action was on the "winner's court." Even if there were more than ten players waiting, plenty to start another game on the adjacent court, no one would leave the winner's court. That is where everyone believed the premiere game was being played and you didn't want to lose your spot in line to play there. The games often included ex-high school basketball players and scholarship football players exercising on their off days for fun. After playing for a few months, I met a couple of regulars who could really play. One of those regulars was Aaron Madry. He had played the previous season on Ohio Northern University's National Championship basketball team, averaging more than twenty points per game in the Final Four. Now living in Columbus, he was a basketball fanatic looking for a game wherever he could find one. He was a 6'2" slasher who could get scorching hot from the perimeter as well. Bottom line: Aaron could flat out score. I hadn't seen many players that good except for maybe K. C. Hunt.

K. C. was a 6'2" point guard who played his first three years of college at Wichita State University. He was a two-time captain and finished in the top ten in school history in steals and assists. He told me he had transferred to Ohio State to finish his playing career, but for some reason it didn't work out. Their loss was my gain because I got to play against him almost every day on the open courts. He is still one of the fiercest competitors I have ever faced. He has always been one of those guys you love to have on your team, but hate to play against.

Nearly every day I showed up at Larkins Hall, I tried to find Aaron or K. C. If I was able to pair up with either, we could potentially play for hours without losing. If they were teamed up against me, mine would be a short day. Why? When a team lost, three or more teams waited to play on the winner's court. With this lengthy wait time and no officials, there was a continual debate over crucial calls and no calls. This translated into intense play with frequent trash talking, arguing, and even fights. If I weren't a competitive player before, this environment brought out a fire I didn't know I had.

Win or go home. Period.

Ask any of the players who played at Larkins Hall, and they will tell you it was a basketball battle ground. I found the best time to play exceptional competition was early Saturday mornings. While most of campus slept, Larkins Hall let anyone with a pulse into the facility to play. Almost none of the players who came then were enrolled, and they all seemed to play angry at the world. As usual, losers could expect to sit for at least an hour before getting another chance. All the extra bodies jammed into the un-air-conditioned gym waiting for their turn sent the heat index into triple digits. All the players waiting for their turns hooted and hollered from the sidelines. This atmosphere was entirely foreign to me, having grown up playing coach guided open gyms in my small suburban community. I was getting an education I didn't expect in my time at OSU—a street ball education.

When I wasn't finding a pick-up game, I was looking for tickets to watch the Buckeyes. I bought a half-season pass and watched games from the roof of St. John Arena, three rows from the top in Section 13B. From this perch, I watched the Buckeyes' victory over rival Indiana. The curvature of the arena roof combined with the volume of the hysterical crowd reverberated through the facility creating a deafening experience and a defining moment for that season.

Overall, the Buckeyes' record was subpar during my freshman year, but the team showed outstanding potential for the future. Two of their most promising players, Derek Anderson and Greg Simpson, were sophomores leading a talented list of returning players. Anderson was a slashing guard from Kentucky who could score like crazy and fly off the floor. The Wildcats had definitely missed on not recruiting him. As a high school senior, he was Kentucky's runner-up Mr. Basketball and seemed to be out to prove he should have won that award. He was my favorite of all the promising young talent.

Simpson, a McDonald's All American from Lima, Ohio, was one of only a handful of players in the state high school history to be named Mr. Basketball twice. He was also freshman of the year in the Big Ten, proving his high school accolades weren't a fluke. He looked to be an All Big Ten, All American-type player for years to come. Other college basketball programs would have jumped at the chance to get a player of his caliber.

Then there was Charles Macon, who was a McDonald's All American from Michigan City, Indiana. I often heard people call him "Killer Macon" for reasons unknown to me. Maybe it had to do with the way he played, because he was exceptional at times. As a senior, he was Mr. Basketball in Indiana, which made it all the more impressive that Ohio State had stolen him away from the likes of Indiana and Purdue. Being named Mr. Basketball in Indiana generally means the player is destined for stardom, and Macon showed glimpses of this early on in Columbus.

If that weren't enough talent, the team snatched up Gerald Eaker, a 6'11" raw athlete from hallowed St. Joseph's High School in Chicago, Illinois. That high school gained fame in the 1994 movie *Hoop Dreams*. Eaker was long and mobile with a "sky is the limit" feel to his potential. He saw the court sparingly that first season because he played behind 6'9" Lawrence Funderburke, a senior forward who went on to play in the NBA for a number of years. It appeared Eaker would slide into the starting lineup nicely the next season. The future looked bright for the Buckeye hoops squad. I envisioned watching them grow and compete for Big Ten titles throughout my college experience.

I finished my freshman year and headed back to Canfield that summer to work as a custodian by day and to umpire baseball with my friend Chris at night. Like many college students, I worked thirteen-hour days to earn money for my housing the next school year. Little did I know that my normal college student life was about to change dramatically.

HELP WANTED

The fall of 1994 brought a return to Columbus for my sophomore year. Having a lot of the freshman unknowns out of the way, I came back ready to hit the ground running. Classwork, pick-up basketball games, and officiating intramural volleyball filled my days. Things were moving along as anticipated until about three weeks into fall quarter when my path took an unexpected turn.

While sitting in a campus dining hall eating lunch between classes, I glanced at the school newspaper, *The Lantern*. A student interest piece about the basketball team caught my eye. The more I read, the more intriguing the article became because it detailed some eye-opening commotion that had transpired within the Buckeye basketball program during the off season.

While I was home scraping gum off desks at C. H. Campbell Elementary School during the day and calling balls and strikes during double headers at night, the talented young nucleus of the Buckeye hoops squad had been busy as well.

Where to start? Let's begin with the 911 call.

In the early morning of July 19, Antonio Watson, a rising senior, called 911 to report that Gerald Eaker had shot one of the tires on Antonio's car. Almost immediately, Eaker was dismissed from the team. Riding with Eaker in the car was teammate Greg Simpson, who already had impaired driving charges against him from the previous March. This additional concern led the athletic department to immediately suspend Simpson. Greg would run into trouble again in September as everyone was returning to campus. His girlfriend filed charges of domestic violence against him. Following this incident, Simpson was dismissed from the team.

That sounds like plenty to deal with for one basketball program during one summer, but this was only part of the Buckeye basketball program's problems. Charles Macon also ran into trouble when felony theft and marijuana possession charges were brought against him. He spent ten days working on a road crew in his home state of Indiana as a result. Macon eventually flunked out of school, leaving the team with yet another black eye.

The fallout didn't end there. Nate Wilbourne, the 6'10"junior from nearby Upper Arlington High School, decided he needed a fresh start, as did Derek Anderson. Wilbourne transferred to the University of South Carolina, and Anderson left for Kentucky. Neither wanted to deal with the chaos surrounding the program and headed for what they hoped would be better basketball lives. To add to the mounting concerns, the Ohio State program was on probation for recruiting violations, so the team was permitted one less scholarship than usual.

What did all this translate into? Huge question marks as to how the Buckeyes would fill out a roster and win games during the 1994–1995 season. The team included several dual sport players, like John Lumpkin, who was on a football scholarship, and Otis Winston, who was on a track scholarship, to help fill some of those spots. But after all the transfers and dismissals, the program still needed players. I kept reading the article intently, hanging onto every word. The last paragraph stated that the Buckeyes might have to add walk-ons.

The wheels in my brain started turning. They needed walk-ons, or players who were students on campus. I was a student on campus. I played basketball all the time and would pretty much cut off my right arm to play on the team. I kept thinking. Whom had I played against on campus who was better than me? Guys like Aaron Madry and K. C. Hunt were really good but out of eligibility. Everyone else I had seen seemed pretty similar to me, and who even knew if they would try out? I got it in my head to give it a shot. Why not? What is the worst that could happen? If nothing else, trying out was a chance to say I played in St. John Arena once, right?

I completed my physical and turned in the paperwork. I showed up for the two-hour evening tryout session hoping to get at least a decent story to tell out of the whole experience. I walked into St. John Arena not knowing what to expect other than nervous anticipation.

TRYING OUT

When I walked in, so did the rest of campus. Anyone who was a student could show up, and it seemed they did. They all must have read the same article I had. One guy came with super short shorts, knee high socks, and enough head and wrist bands to stop any perspiration from ever leaving his body. Even with a few attention seekers in attendance, plenty of players with good size, athletic builds and all business facial expressions showed up. My stomach twisted in knots as I scoped out the competition.

I started counting all the students and decided to quit when I got into triple digits. I thought to myself, *How are all these guys going to try out? St. John Arena isn't that big!* Regardless of the high number, we began the session with basic drills like speed dribbling and pivoting. I was amazed how many guys were terrible at these fundamental elements of the game. I could pivot all day thanks to Coach Cullen and all of his youth camps. I tried intently to be as technically sound as possible. I thought maybe that was the separation piece that would get me noticed. As I looked around, I started to gain some confidence that I might have found an edge.

That confidence carried over into the next drill. We paired up to do some one-on-one zig-zag dribbling against a defender. I was paired with a guy named Don Jantonio, who was a 6'2", strong, athletic, cerebral guard from Mentor, Ohio. Don came to Ohio State to play quarterback and played a year of football before he decided it wasn't for him. He was an extremely talented basketball player whom I had never seen before that moment. What benefited me was that Don had never seen me play before either. When it was our turn, I asked one of OSU's assistant coaches watching our drill if we were supposed to beat the defender off the dribble if we could. He said, "Hell yes!" So, I took one jab step right and then blew past Don to the left, leaving him in the dust. Don probably would have given me real trouble had he known I was left handed. Regardless, I had just cruised passed a quality guard.

I hoped the coaches saw that!

How in the world would they efficiently eliminate so many players and when? At the time, it seemed nearly impossible to narrow the field in what seemed like organized chaos. As the end of the session neared, the coaches sat all the players down and read off about twenty names. My name was on the list. We played what amounted to a glorified open gym game while the coaching staff looked on. The rest of the students were relegated to watching.

As the game concluded, the coaching staff pulled everyone together and read off a shorter list. Before reading the names, the coaches said that these players should return at 6:00 a.m. the next morning for a second tryout session. When I heard my name called, a huge feeling of relief came over me. Still, it was hard to believe they cut us down from a small army of players to a handful in a matter of two hours.

Sleep didn't come easily that night as I anticipated the early morning practice. No doubt more cuts were ahead. I showed up at St. John Arena at 5:30 a.m. the next morning. Guys were lacing up their shoes in total silence while anticipating what was to come. We were all trying to make a basketball team most only dreamed of playing on, and we had no idea how many spots were even available.

The session was a blur of fundamentals, defending, rebounding, games, and most notably, nerves. I felt in my gut they weren't looking for flash, so I tried to stay sound and unselfish. The gym had an air of hope and cautious optimism. It was a tremendous display of determination; everyone flew around the gym at 110 miles an hour in an effort to catch a coach's eye. The tryout was a moving experience. In the end, an overwhelming feeling of mutual admiration rose from all the players.

After the coaches pulled us all in again to tell us their decision, they read aloud three names: Don Jantonio, Jerry White, and Eric Hanna. I had survived the walk-on portion of the tryout. To know I was one of the best players at the school with the largest enrollment in the country was tremendously gratifying. Now I would have the opportunity to compete with the team to see if I was worth keeping around.

A WHOLE NEW WORLD

Later that morning, the coaches had us go back over to the offices upstairs in St. John Arena to fill out more paperwork.

All the people working in the offices, the student managers and administrative assistants, acted as if they already knew me. I thought to myself, *How do these people have any idea who I am? I barely played in high school.* They treated me as if I were some prize recruit. It was fun to feel like a celebrity for even a few minutes. The student managers, most of whom were excellent former high school players in their own right, gave me looks of wonder and awe. At the same time, I was thinking, *Dude, I am probably more like you than the guys on scholarship.* All I had done thus far was show I was one of the better student players on campus. I hadn't spent a minute playing with or against the actual team. That experience was going to tell the real story of whether I would be around for any length of time. No one had guaranteed me anything.

Before I could even process the entirety of the situation, the three of us were practicing with the team. Now I was competing with guys I had watched the previous year from the cheap seats. I knew the level of play was going to be higher, but I had no idea how much. The speed, size, strength, and quickness of the players was something I had never experienced. One play, in particular, early in that first practice summed up this whole new world I had entered.

We were scrimmaging, and I was on defense guarding Antonio Watson. Antonio, or Tony as everyone called him, was a 6'9", 250-pound post player from Columbus East High School. He was a third team *Parade* All American coming out of high school who was now a senior and one of the key returnees for the Buckeyes. He was cemented on the block and I was in a help defense position awaiting the next move.

That move came when Carlos Davis, a brash, prized freshman guard from Eastmoor Academy in Columbus, drove right down the middle of the lane. My job was to stop him from getting all the way to the rim. I anticipated he would dish the ball off to Tony, so I decided to fake hard at Carlos and recover back to Tony. When he would go up to shoot, I would go up to try to block it. I thought I was in good help defensive position. I was right. I thought Carlos would drop the ball off to Tony. I was right. I thought I could recover to stop Tony from finishing the play.

I was dead wrong.

When Carlos dished it off, I turned and flew at Tony to try to block his shot attempt. Tony jumped about ten inches higher than I thought possible, and he dunked the ball over me, or what felt like through me. I don't believe I have ever been a part of a more humbling moment in basketball. Thank the good Lord the play was not in an actual game, for I would have been on ESPN's top ten plays and a poster in some eight-year-old's bedroom for the rest of time. The play illustrated how foreign I was to my new basketball environment. I couldn't help but hope I wasn't the only walk-on who was this out of sorts.

I figured out quickly that Don Jantonio wasn't wide eyed like I was. His year with the Ohio State football program helped him understand the expectations, talent level, and mental aspect of Division I college athletics. He adjusted quickly. The other walk-on, Jerry White, was a 6'2" junior guard from Lorain Admiral King High School in Cleveland. He was physically mature, strong, and quick, which allowed him to compete. He was a tough-minded, intelligent engineering student, but his basketball knowledge and skill were raw, so he struggled at times with drills, positioning, and set plays. I couldn't help but gain comfort knowing I wasn't the only guy who didn't have it all together. Still, I was going to have to step up my game to make this team.

ACADEMIC BALANCE

Before I even worried about making the team, I needed to figure out a way to make it to practice. I had no idea I'd be trying out for the basketball team, let alone making it this far, so I hadn't aligned my classes with any basketball practice schedules. Practices were from 3:30 p.m. to 5:30 p.m. every day, and I had Sociology 101 at that exact time. I had to find a way to switch that class time, or else I wouldn't be able to practice. I couldn't skip class every day, or I would surely fail the course. I couldn't drop the class because that would give me only ten hours, and students needed twelve hours to be full-time. Signing up for a new course wasn't an option because it was too late in the quarter to add a class. I had to be full-time to play and practice, so this left me in a tight spot. Was I really going to have to stop pursuing my dream because I couldn't switch my class schedule? I was going to have to think outside the box to make this work.

The Sociology 101 class took place in a giant lecture hall on Mondays, Wednesdays, and Fridays. Hundreds of students took endless notes as our professor spewed information from start to finish. The professor and teachers' assistants (TAs) had no idea which students were there because they never took attendance. Anyone off the street who wanted to learn could have walked in and listened, and no one would have known they weren't a student. I wouldn't be penalized for skipping those sessions other than missing out on the material. I would have to learn the information by reading on my own or getting notes from other students.

The real problem was Tuesdays and Thursdays when we had the recitation portion of class. Our teaching assistant led about thirty students who interacted throughout the session. The TA took attendance and expected students to be there as a class requirement. I had to find a way to make this work, or my basketball experience would be over.

I went to meet with the TA during office hours to discuss options. She said it was too late in the quarter to switch sections because we had already started our group projects. She also said I needed the material from these sections to complete the class. I got a huge lump in my throat. *This is the end,* I thought. *This is it.* My chance of making the team appeared to be gone, not because I wasn't good enough, but because of my schedule. We had to be able to make something work. I needed an option that would let me do both. I was willing to work hard and desperate to find a plan that would let me keep going.

Something? Anything?

Fortunately, my TA was realistic and understanding but in no way unethical. She came up with a solution. She said that the group project was not an issue because my group would already be arranging to meet at times that were outside of the class schedule and those times would have to work for all students in the group, including me. This would satisfy the project portion of the class. To make up for the missed recitation, I would meet with her during her office hours twice each week to discuss the class material. It didn't sound easy, but the plan sounded doable because her office hours fit into my now frenetic schedule.

The next week, I began meeting with my TA. The first time I showed up, she seemed almost surprised I came. Who knows if she thought I would blow it off or if she forgot we had even made the plan? Either way, I was ready to discuss the material. The meeting went relatively smoothly, although I was really uncomfortable having a one-on-one class. Awkward or not, the plan was working.

The second time I showed up to her office hours, ready to discuss the material from that week, we talked briefly. Then she said something I didn't expect, "Well, you have shown a good grasp of the material. I don't think you have to come to my office hours anymore unless you have specific questions."

Really? I thought to myself. *I'm supposed to show up for the midterm and the final and do this on my own?* I was basically taking a class I wasn't even attending. Could I really pull this off? Initially, this didn't sound like a path to academic success. Regardless, I had found a way to make the class fit. I could attend full-time and continue to go through the basketball tryout process. Neither part of the equation sounded like it was going to be easy.

HAVE I MADE IT?

As soon as I was able to make arrangements to continue to tryout, I returned to practice. I wish I could say that I felt much better with my scheduling conflicts resolved, but this wasn't the case. My head was spinning. I wasn't used to playing this level of basketball. Not only was it mentally taxing during practice because everything was happening so much faster, but not knowing where I stood with making the team continually caused me stress.

I needed support during the process. So, I started with a phone call to my mom after every practice. Every night I made a similar statement, "Hi, Mom. Yes, I am still practicing with the team, but I will probably get cut tomorrow." It wasn't that I knew anything about their plans, it was more about my lack of confidence. I also called Coach Cullen for advice and words of encouragement. I could feel the excitement in his voice when we spoke. The way he talked, his teachings and program were trying out with me. I felt a sense of pride because I was representing my community, but his hopes also added to the pressure to succeed.

When I asked for advice, Coach Cullen had a very clear message; I needed to play with "no respect for my body." Translation: I needed to dive for every loose ball, grab every rebound, and not worry about injury while making every hustle play possible. I tried to channel his words into reality. I felt my effort was deserving of a place on the team. Hustle was one thing, but the question that kept entering my mind was, "Do they really need me?"

I believed I had a good understanding of our set plays and drills. At a height of 6'7 1/2" wearing shoes, decent mobility, and a solid skill set, I could be plugged in wherever they needed a body. Still, I was terrified to ask if they were keeping me. It wasn't as if they would have cut me for asking, yet I didn't have the moxie to say anything. So, I waited for a sign or subtle hint to tell me I had made the team.

PICTURE THIS

In my mind, the first event that would undoubtedly tell me if I had made the team was picture day. If I was in the team picture, I must be on the team, right? When picture day arrived, nervous energy consumed me. I couldn't help but wonder if I would have a jersey in my locker or a pink slip waiting there instead.

When I arrived at the arena that day, I went down the multi-door hallway that led to the varsity locker room and then turned the corner to the players' dressing area. My heart was thumping so vigorously it was as if the Ohio State Marching Band drums were pulsating in the stands above and reverberating into the locker room and throughout my body. With nervous energy building, I was seconds away from knowing. I had put a lot of work into my dream, and I was about to find out my fate.

I turned another corner, looked into my locker, and saw a jersey. After a huge sigh of relief, I took a closer look that curbed my excitement. The jersey had "Anderson" on the back. Derek Anderson obviously wasn't showing up for pictures after he transferred to Kentucky. While this clearly wasn't my jersey, it seemed I was to put it on because it was hanging in my locker. So, with much confusion, I started getting dressed.

I thought about the situation while I changed, and I came to one conclusion. It didn't matter what was written on the back of the jersey, it mattered only that I had a jersey. No one was going to be taking pictures from behind us. The name on the back was unimportant. What mattered was the name on the front. On the front of the jersey OHIO STATE was clear. I had a jersey to wear in the picture.

This was it! I was really on the team!

I happened to see that Don and Jerry both had jerseys with former players' names on the back as well. Don had number thirty-five with Eaker written on it. Jerry had number three with Simpson where his last name should have been. I thought they must have run out of time to make jerseys for the walk-ons and gave us old ones so we could be in the picture. Jerry and I kidded about the names that obviously were not ours. I started to feel more at ease.

While we waited, I realized two new players I had forgotten about would be joining us. Ricky Dudley and John Lumpkin both played tight end on the football team, so they hadn't been practicing with us yet. They would join the team after the bowl game. That would likely be in January.

First the photographer took individual pictures. My spirits rose. Each of us stood in front of a gray screen for headshots. All the guys were excited and clowned around. This was the good stuff. We had done all the hard work over the past few weeks to get to this reward. It was a nice change to think we were doing something as a team other than grinding through another preseason practice, forgetting for a moment that would begin again as soon as the photo shoot was over. At that moment, we were to commemorate the 1994–1995 Ohio State men's basketball team with a photo, and I couldn't wait to be in it.

The photographers wrapped up individual pictures and began to line everyone up for the team photo. Just as we began to line up, one of the assistant coaches, Randy Roth, came over to talk to Don, Jerry, and me. He said they had decided to hold us out of the team picture at this point.

Keep us out of the team picture? What?

I did not see this coming. My mind started racing again. Since I took the individual picture, I assumed I was on the team. Maybe I'm not? All the team needed to do was scrap my individual picture, and I'd be erased from the program. They could say, "Thanks for getting us through the preseason. See you later!" Suddenly, I'd be gone from memory. As on top of the world as I was minutes before, I felt like the world rolled over me and crushed my basketball existence.

Steamrolled.

What made things even harder was that Ricky Dudley and John Lumpkin were smiling with uniforms on, lining up straight and tall, and laughing with all the other guys in the team picture. I could give Ricky a pass. He had been a player on the team for the past three years and had earned his spot. Ricky had been Texas Class 4A Player of the Year in football in high school and decided he wanted to play both sports after three years of basketball. John, on the other hand (who by the way was a great guy and a great teammate), was the one who struck a nerve at that moment because he was a freshman who had never run a single sprint inside St. John Arena in his life. Here I was tearing my guts out every day during practice and standing on the sideline. Meanwhile, he wore a uniform with his name on it, and he was in the team photo. When the pictures were over, John would walk out and head back to football for a couple months while we threw on our sweaty practice gear and got beat up for another punishing three-hour preseason practice session that at times felt more like a battle of wills than an attempt to get better at basketball.

Couldn't they take multiple team pictures with all of us collectively so that if we made the team the photo might actually reflect everyone from that season? I felt like I was getting cut right then and there, as if I were being erased from existence like in the movie *Back to the Future*, when Michael J. Fox watched himself vanish from a photo he held in his hands. All of this was going through my mind while they took the last few snap shots. As the photo shoot wound down and all the players began to head into the locker room to change for practice, I felt used. I was at a loss for words.

Fortunately, Don Jantonio was not. His time with the football program helped him understand how expendable walk-ons were to coaches, so he spoke up. Don stopped Coach Roth and asked him the question Jerry and I were also thinking: *When are you going to know if we made the team or not?* Coach Roth paused for a second and said, "You'll probably know Friday."

For the moment, I got what I badly needed. This gave me a timeline with an end in sight. The hard part was I had a disheartening answer to the question of whether I had made the team. I hadn't made it yet. All of my sweat and hard work might not pay off. I had gotten my hopes up after working through my class conflicts and putting my body through the physical and emotional drains of preseason practice. It would be a tough pill to swallow if I got cut now. I tried to stay optimistic. The fact that there were more practices ahead still gave me a chance to impress the coaches and make the team, right?

FRIDAY NIGHT FLIGHT

I was a bundle of nerves during the practices up to and including Friday. I frequently turned the ball over and shot poorly. I put forth the physical effort, but I was beating myself up mentally. As practice ended Friday, I thought it was only a matter of time until the coaches called me over to tell me they didn't need me anymore. I was desperately trying to hold on to some control in the situation, so I decided to make cutting me hard for them. If I left the gym quickly so they didn't get a chance to talk to me, then they couldn't cut me, at least not today.

This was obviously a ridiculous plan, but I was panicked, and I didn't want to face the potential truth of not being good enough. As soon as we broke huddle, I headed toward the locker room as quickly as I could without looking odd. I tried hard not to make eye contact with any coaches as I exited. I felt weird being the first guy in the locker room, as I usually stayed after to shoot. Once I was in there, I set a speed record for showering and changing clothes. Then I headed for the equipment room to drop off my sweaty practice gear.

After bag drop, players went back through the gym and up the ramp on the opposite side of the arena to exit. The coaches often stood and talked after practice, either in the gym or on that ramp. They frequently chatted with players who headed out. That was the last place on earth I wanted to go. If they could see me, they could cut me. I went the opposite direction. I jetted past the equipment room, past the girls' basketball and volleyball locker rooms, and headed up a stairwell I never knew existed.

The narrow staircase twisted and turned until it funneled me out of the arena. I was so happy to be outside I didn't even care where I was. I made it out of the arena undetected like an escaped convict. I looked up and saw I was on the Lane Avenue side of the arena looking at the Varsity Club across the street. This was the opposite side of where I wanted to be, but I didn't care because I had avoided the coaches. I was safe for the moment.

Now that I am a lot older and hopefully wiser, I look back and laugh at that moment. I should have simply asked so I didn't keep questioning where I stood. Then I could have moved on either way. Even when I showed up for the next practice, no one told me to go home, and no one told me I had made it. I was still left wondering and worrying if I was really on the team.

SUIT UP?

I believed my next chance for a definitive answer about my playing status would come the following week when we were to play our first scrimmage. At that time, Division I teams scrimmaged semipro squads in front of fans. We would play in uniform like it was an official game with broadcasts on local television networks. If I was in a uniform that night, it would clearly mean I was on the team, right?

Head coach, Randy Ayers, pulled us together at the end of a practice early that week to discuss the schedule for the day of the scrimmage. This exhibition game also gave the team a chance to get used to a pregame routine. He began to rattle off instructions and, at times, peered at the ceiling as if the answers were written there. Coach Ayers told us we would meet for a pregame meal four hours before game time. We also would meet in the locker room an hour and a half prior to tip off.

Along with the timing of the events, he mentioned we should all wear a suit to the game. Immediately I began to worry because I didn't have a suit. I'd never owned a suit in my life. I wore a dress shirt and a tie to any formal occasion while growing up, but suits were expensive, so they really weren't an option. This posed a problem for me, so I quickly decided I had to ask about it. For the first time the entire preseason, I opened my mouth in front of everyone at practice. I raised my hand, and when Coach Ayers called on me, this is how the conversation went.

Me: "What if you don't own a suit?"

Coach Ayers: "Don't come."

And, at that, the conversation was over. I felt like someone had sucker punched me in the gut. This reinforced why I was wise to keep my mouth shut. I felt like if I ever said anything else, I probably would have been shown the exit. Now, I definitely didn't feel like I meant much to the program. I decided I would never again speak at basketball practice. Thankfully, assistant coach Jerry Francis was there to talk me out of becoming a mime. He pulled me aside after that and said some words of encouragement telling me I had a few days to get things together before the game.

The next day, I looked at suits. I bought two, figuring I could use them for job interviews someday even if the basketball thing didn't work out. The sales person measured and fitted me for a rush order that I could pick up on game day. At least I could attend the game. Whether I would be in a uniform or watching in a dark gray suit was yet to be determined. I certainly wasn't going to open my mouth and ask anything again for fear of being told to never come back.

The day of the scrimmage, we went to our pregame meal and headed into our locker room an hour and a half before game time. I walked down the hallway into the players' area, swung around the corner, and peered into my locker to see what, if anything, was in there.

Nothing.

My stomach flipped. No uniform at all? Heck, I would have settled for one with someone else's name on it. What made the void deeper was Don Jantonio actually had a jersey in his locker with his name on it, and he played in the game! All the while, Jerry White and I sat at the end of the bench in suits. No one talked to us about our situation, and I was not going to ask.

Behaving like a team player that night was difficult, mostly because I still didn't even know if I was on the team. Don's dressing and playing made me wonder even more about my status. I started to think they would just keep me in a suit until the football players were finished with their bowl game, and then they'd cast me off like I had never been there for the first five weeks of preseason. I had been tearing my guts out trying to get better, and I still didn't feel like I belonged. I envisioned a future where I didn't even mention the try out because it would sound something like this:

Someone says to me, "Wow, you're tall. Do you play basketball?"

I say, "Yes."

They ask, "Where?"

I say, "I played at Ohio State for a season."

They reply, "Oh really? When?"

I answer, "1994–1995."

They ask, "Did you play a lot?"

I say, "No, I never got to dress for a game."

They query, "I don't understand. Did you really play or not?"

Unless something changed, it sounded like a horribly vague and fabricated story, so I imagined I would never talk about this experience. Who would believe me? People tell these kinds of stories all the time whether they are true or not. They offer few facts and little to no proof. People would question not only the story but my integrity as well.

I was pretty beaten down, physically and emotionally. Still, I showed up for practice and kept battling. I had learned a lot from my year away from the team in high school. Mostly I learned I loved basketball. If I wasn't playing with the team, I would have been playing the same number of days on an open court somewhere on campus with less talented opponents and no coaching. So, I fought on and hoped maybe things would change. The second exhibition game came and went with me sitting on the bench again, this time in the forest green sport coat and navy blue dress pants I had also purchased. I persisted. I held my head up in hopes that the coaches would recognize my resiliency. Even if the coaching staff didn't recognize it, I hoped something would make me feel like a member of the team.

FULL CIRCLE

I believed my final chance to be an official member of the team and not just a practice body would come when we played our season opener. We played in the preseason

National Invitational Tournament (NIT) against Ohio University, which boasted one of the best teams in school history. They arguably had the best player in school history in Gary Trent. People called him the "Shaq of the MAC," comparing his dominance over the Mid-American Conference to that of Shaquille O'Neil. Trent played at Hamilton Township High School and set a national record his senior year, shooting 81.4 percent for the season. You could be in the gym all by yourself and not shoot that well! They also had Geno Ford, the second all-time leading scorer in Ohio High School Athletic Association history at that time with 2,680 points during his high school career. He had a tremendous leadership quality and toughness to win. This would be a tough game for sure.

We prepped for several days leading up to the game. We watched film of them and studied a detailed scouting report. I enjoyed planning and strategizing how to beat an opponent. Although I was excited about the team finally playing a game that counted, I couldn't help but wonder whether my personal role would change as the real season began.

Game day finally arrived. We attended our now routine pregame meal. Like clockwork, we showed up at the arena ninety minutes before the game. I made the long walk through the locker room and down the narrow hallway wondering if I would see the same empty locker. As I made the turn, I held my breath.

Please let there be a jersey in there ... please.

I looked into my locker and a uniform hung there. It was too good to be true. I wondered if it was the same uniform I had worn picture day. I grabbed it out of my locker, took it off the hanger, and spun it around. This time, in big bold letters on the back, was "HANNA."

I paused for a moment. I had a jersey. All the extra practice had paid off. I had a jersey. The stress and sacrifice of my body was all for this. I had a jersey. I had forgone class and taught myself a collegiate sociology course from a textbook, all for this moment! I had a jersey with my name on it. I had proof I was part of this program. I had made The Ohio State University basketball team.

If the fact that I had a jersey at all wasn't amazing enough, there was another connection no one could have predicted. I thought back to high school. I thought back to Coach Cullen saying, *"Eric's going to be a heck of a player when he is twenty."* I thought back to attending the state tournament and watching our conference rivals win the state title that our team so badly coveted. I remembered the void I felt, thinking my career was over. As we left the tournament, I had bought a Woody Hayes "Block O" style hat and a basketball jersey. I had purchased a number twenty-three jersey because I really thought Derek Anderson would be a great player for the Buckeyes for years to come. I was partially right. He was a great player—for Kentucky. He played on their 1996 national championship team the following season. When he left Ohio State, no new players were given that number until now. When I looked below my name, screen printed on the back was number twenty-three.

How ironic. At the moment I thought signified the end of my career, I actually purchased the jersey I would wear less than two years later when I found my way back into the game. Words can only begin to describe the joy of this moment, and nothing can touch the twist of fate. I went from a player who was barely good enough to be on his high school team to making The Ohio State University basketball roster.

I never ran through warm-ups that night, I floated. I was in heaven as we ran out onto the court, and I heard The

Ohio State University Marching Band play our fight song. The sound of 13,276 fans cheering at a fevered pitch for our team was a euphoria I had never known before and will never forget. I didn't play a second that night, but the collective experience more than made up for that. I was finally in a uniform and ready if called upon.

CHAPTER 5
Survival Mode

During my freshman year, I frequently saw athletes around campus wearing letterman's jackets when everyone walked to class. I always wondered what sport they played because all jackets had the same "Block O" but no sport distinction. I also wondered why they all walked so slowly. Were they just too cool to move at the same pace as everyone else? After I started playing, I found out why. Athletes were too tired to move any faster!

Our practices were beyond physically demanding. The grueling sessions produced exhaustion and bruising that made each afternoon seem more like a street brawl. To survive, I needed mental toughness, physical bulk, and strength. Sadly, I was deficient in all these. Standing at 6'7½" helped, but my 175-pound frame was my kryptonite. By high school standards, that was considered extremely slender. For a Big Ten player, my build was unfathomable. From the start, every day was a back-alley fight, and every day I left beat up. Sometimes walking slowly on campus was the only break I felt like I ever had.

We started most practices by stretching and warming up with running/ball handling drills. Then we broke off into guard and post player workouts. That was when the physical punishment ramped up. I went with the post players, meaning I would spend the next thirty minutes trying to stop the largest players on our team from rooting themselves next to the basket and shoving me into next week so they could shoot uncontested lay-ups. The Big Ten had a reputation at the time of being a big, plodding, physical league. Our practices were designed to prepare us for that stereotype. We played one-on-one in the post for huge chunks of time and coaches didn't call fouls, mostly to keep us moving and playing. Every single post player outweighed me by at least forty pounds, so every hit took a considerable toll on my body.

One drill included all post players at once, no fouls, no timeouts, and no breaks until a player scored three baskets. Once we scored three times, we could come out. From the onset, the other players didn't realize how physical the drill allowed them to be. I managed to score two early buckets before anyone else. I thought to myself, *I'm going to win this drill. I needed only one more basket, one lucky break, or one more bounce to go my way.* As the drill continued, durability became a factor. Players hacked, clawed, and bounced each other around to get any rebound they could. Fatigue set in. I couldn't consistently match the mass of the other players for an extended length of time.

One by one, each player made their third basket and consequently exited the drill. Eventually, the only player still in the drill was me. I was so fatigued I could barely stand. I must have looked like I had just left a prize fight, as the loser of course. I felt beaten, demoralized, and broken down. In one drill, all my shortcomings as a player had been summed up. I had very little chance of playing because my body couldn't take the pounding. At this stage, it wasn't even about getting on the court in games; it was about staying healthy and strong enough to be on the court in practice.

My general bruising was so bad, our trainers got a new idea to protect me. Because I didn't carry much bulk on my frame, they decided we should fabricate some. They started having me wear a football girdle during practice, complete with hip and tailbone pads, to protect me from injuries in everyday post play. This was perfect irony. I felt like I was playing football, so why not wear football pads, right? If I didn't change something, my body wasn't going to survive into the new calendar year.

No one else wore pads, so I wasn't thrilled about it. I caught flak from a few guys when I changed for practice one day. The padding was embarrassing. For the amount it helped, the protection didn't seem worth the ridicule. For several weeks, even while wearing the pads, I grimaced every time I had to hip check anyone. I cheered inside when a player I was guarding went out on the perimeter because that gave my body a break.

How ironic that nowadays players voluntarily buy girdles for basketball. I frequently see players wearing compression shorts to prevent hip and thigh bruises. Not only are the pads in these clothes much softer, but they flow considerably better with body movement. On top of providing improved comfort, they are even fashionable. Too bad I wasn't able to cash in on the growth of the product, because I was the one forced to wear padding before it was comfortable or cool!

Regardless of the pads, the poundings continued. As if it wasn't bad enough to get a physical beating from the post players, the guards weighed in as well. One player got so frustrated with Coach Ayers verbally riding him all the time and me screening him to try to get his man open that he decided he would run through me every time I went near him in practice. My job was to keep setting screens and doing so resulted in a scuffle that our coaches eventually broke up. It's a good thing too, because that player would have broken me in half. The same guy tormented Jerry and me when we shot after practice, telling us it was a waste of time. The taunting fueled our fire to get better.

WEIGHT GAME

Before walking on and making the basketball team, I never went into a college weight room voluntarily. I think I was once coerced inside by my roommates during my freshman year, and I couldn't wait to leave. Now that I was playing on the team, I didn't have a choice. Every day I cringed inside when we headed toward the weight facility. That was the last place on earth I wanted to go. As we headed over, I must have appeared physically ill.

I had lifted weights in high school and hated every minute of it. I wasn't just bad at lifting; I was the worst on our team by far. The weights seemed to reject me. I always endured debilitating soreness, and I never felt like I was getting stronger. Even worse, the next time we lifted, I still suffered pain from the previous session. I wondered how I was supposed to practice basketball while I was so sore. Once inside the weight room, I feared nothing more than the bench press.

When a person lifts weights, the first question anyone ever asks is, "How much do you bench?" Bench press weight was the true measure of manliness. The problem for me was every player on the team could bench so much more than I could, it was laughable. My lifting partner would get an extra workout while changing the weight on the bar between sets because I benched so much less. I didn't want to go near the bench because it was so embarrassing. I knew I had to lift to get stronger, but I didn't need anyone watching.

I can remember one workout session being particularly terrifying. I began, as I frequently did, doing curls, leg extensions, or anything but bench press. I did that last, when everyone else had cleared out. On this specific day, Coach Langworthy, our strength coach, saw that we had guys all over the weight room at different stages of their workout. He said we should be lifting as a team so we could bond. I didn't mind bonding, but not here.

I reluctantly went over to the benches and ended up right next to Ricky Dudley and John Lumpkin. I began to set up my bench as always, finding two tens to put on either side of the bar for a total of eighty-five pounds. This is a quality amount of weight to bench press if you are an eighth-grade cross country runner. I was a sophomore in college playing in the Big Ten. That weight was like the punch line of a joke.

Ricky and John used a slightly different amount to start. They grabbed three plates and placed them on each side, carefully balancing the weights so they didn't flip the bar off the bench. They both warmed up with 315 pounds. At that moment, I felt like the weakest individual on the planet, and we hadn't even started. My insecurity got worse when I needed someone to spot me to finish my sets. One of my teammates lifted the weight off of me with one arm when I ran out of gas. The experience was mortifying. I tried to keep in mind that both of these guys were football players who could lift with anyone. Ricky was built like an action figure, and John could be described only as a mountain of a man. Still, I couldn't help but feel I was outclassed by everyone around me.

Despite how discouraging the exercise was, I committed myself to the weight room. I had to if I was ever to compete on the court. By the end of the year, I had made substantial gains. I finished the season benching 165 pounds. This was a staggering amount less than everyone else, but I still remember Coach Langworthy saying I had made impressive progress in comparison to where I had started. I would have to continue to make this kind of progress to compete.

BUSTED

As the season progressed, Coach Ayers made every effort to manufacture victories and ensure we abided by the rules. With the recent transgressions of players, we couldn't afford to have any more missteps, especially when victories were going to be so elusive with an undermanned team. Early in the season, Coach Ayers sat us down and gave us a form to fill out. The sheet was to explain to our compliance office where each player had bought their cars, gotten the money to make the payments, who was paying for the insurance, and anything else about loans or money. When Coach Ayers finished talking, Don Jantonio looked at me, laughing, and said "Well, we're busted." I looked back and laughed as well, then said, "Yep, our playing days are over." Kerry Johnson, one of the student managers who hung out with us from time to time also laughed. He said, "Yeah, you guys might as well turn in your uniforms."

The reason we all mocked the requirement was that Don was driving a royal blue, four-door, 1986 Chevy Cavalier. In 1995, people weren't beating down the doors to get that kind of ride. I was sporting a 1985 gun metal gray Buick Skyhawk with a sizable dent in the front fender and a falling ceiling liner. It was exactly what every college kid wasn't looking for in a vehicle. I am pretty certain no booster would have furnished us cars that dilapidated.

Not only was my ride about as unattractive as possible, there was no question where the financing had come from. I had bought it with money I earned delivering papers every Sunday morning from the time I was seven until midway through high school. I felt certain no one on the team would have traded for my car. In fact, I didn't even have a campus parking pass, so I had been biking back and forth to practice anyway (which was an extra workout I didn't need). As Don and I laughed, I couldn't help but think this was one detail I didn't have to get stressed out about.

STAR STRUCK

Every time the lights came on for a game, all the compliance, intense practices, bruises, and effort became worthwhile. It was if I were living in a *Sports Center* highlight that kept airing over and over throughout the season. Players like Gary Trent had me star struck and for good reason. He exhibited why he was an NBA lottery pick, carrying his team not only past us, but all the way to the NIT championship. He wound up being a lottery pick in the NBA draft chosen as the eleventh overall pick by Milwaukee. We soon played Bowling Green State University, who had landed a superstar of their own in Antonio Daniels. He also became a lottery pick, fourth overall, to the Vancouver Grizzlies in 1997.

During our nonconference schedule, it seemed every team we played had NBA talent. The first road game we played was in Philadelphia, and I took the first airplane flight in my life. We played the University of Pennsylvania, and like everyone else, they seemed to have one of their best teams in school history. The Quakers were an NCAA tournament team undefeated in the Ivy League that season, thanks to two future NBA players. Jerome Allen, a second-round pick by the Timberwolves, and Matt Maloney, who would later play six years in the NBA, made the Penn back court as good as any in the country that season.

Both the Quakers and the location for the game were outstanding. The Palestra is arguably the most iconic facility in college basketball. The gym dates back to 1927 and has the distinction of hosting more college basketball games than any other facility. Five Philadelphia teams played their home contests there for decades. Drexel had made five NCAA tournament appearances, Saint Joseph's made the 1961 Final Four, Pennsylvania had made the 1979 Final Four, LaSalle won the 1954 NCAA Championship, and Villanova won the 1985 NCAA Championship while calling the Palestra home. The place was a basketball addict's dream, often the setting for double and triple headers on winter Saturdays.

Heaven on hardwood.

The facility did not disappoint. The 8,722-seat arena sent a cacophony of sound through the ventilation system as if someone put a giant speaker over the chalkboard in our closet-sized locker room. No one could hear Coach Ayers's pregame speech. What we heard instead was Pennsylvania's raucous yet educated fan base, who jeered at our team throughout warm-ups. They hollered statements like, "Are you still in the Big Ten, or are you in the Patriot League now?" With a future NBA backcourt and the Palestra on their side, we got trounced that day, dodging paper airplanes made out of our roster sheets as we exited.

The list of historic facilities, talent and losses piled up. Later that season we played at the storied Wisconsin Field House, where they traditionally threw penny filled marshmallows at opponents. There, we got a firsthand look at Michael Findley, who was a 1995 first round pick by the Phoenix Suns and twenty-first overall. He had the most impressive missed dunk I have ever seen. On a fast break, he took off from the elbow soaring toward the rim. Otis Winston, our 6'6" forward, who still holds the Ohio State outdoor high jump record at 7'4 ½", was running back on defense. Otis leaped and barely got a piece of Findley's elbow as he flew by. Findley hammered the ball off the back of the rim so hard it flew out to half court, where their point guard grabbed it. Our bench was so in awe of the play we stood in frozen wonderment, as did our players on the court. Their point guard quickly collected the ball and fired it inside to Rashard Griffith, the 7'0", 280-pound Wisconsin center who was a 1995 NBA draft pick for the Milwaukee Bucks and thirty-eighth overall. Griffith didn't just dunk the ball, he engulfed the rim. We slowly picked our jaws up off the floor and made a futile search for the dignity lost on the play. At that moment, we knew the game was over. Our season would continue this pattern of losses.

During the 1994–1995 season, we played nine of the fifty-eight players drafted into the NBA that year. If we weren't winning, at least we were getting a chance to play against the best. In addition to the aforementioned teams and players, here is a list of some of the NBA talent that burned us in the remainder of the 1994–95 season.

- Michigan State–Sean Respert (Eighth pick, Portland Trail-blazers) and Eric Snow (Forty-third pick, Milwaukee Bucks)
- Indiana–Alan Henderson (Sixteenth pick, Indiana Pacers)
- Michigan–Jimmy King (Thirty-fifth pick, Toronto Raptors)
- Purdue–Cuonzo Martin (Fifty-seventh pick, Atlanta Hawks)

We found a few fading moments of success during our long road. We defeated the Drexel Dragons, led by Malik Rose (1996 second-round pick by the Charlotte Hornets; two-time NBA champion with the Spurs). We also pulled off a victory against the Minnesota Golden Gophers and Voshon Leonard (1994 second-round pick by the Milwaukee Bucks). Finally, we beat the University of Tennessee–Chattanooga and Terrell Owens. Owens was a pretty solid basketball player for the Moccasins but is better known for his Hall of Fame NFL career. As a member of the 49ers, Eagles, and Cowboys, he was selected first team All-Pro five times and even had his own television show. As a hoops player, his physicality certainly helped him succeed and helped his team make the NCAA tournament that season. In all, we earned three wins against NCAA tournament qualifying teams.

THE BEST OF TIMES

Even if the wins were few and far between, I soaked up all the enjoyment of playing big time college basketball. Sure, I wasn't playing during games, but I was in uniform for all of them, and I consistently looked forward to prepping our team for each upcoming opponent. For example, Iowa ran a gadget play where they had a shooter purposefully come up extra short so a teammate who got the rebound (really a pass) could lay the ball in while the opponent kept looking at the basket, still waiting for the original shot to come off. The "shot lob" play, as it was called, gave our players fits. For a scout team guy like me, plays like this made practice fun.

Possibly the most exciting scouting opportunity came when we were preparing for George Mason University. Legendary head coach Paul Westhead led The Patriots. ESPN made a *30 for 30* episode on him called the "Guru of Go." The episode emphasized Westhead's success with the NBA's Los Angeles Lakers, the Phoenix Mercury WNBA team, and most memorably, Loyola Marymount University in the early 1990s. Coach Westhead's team had a system no one else in college basketball used. Their team would sprint down the floor and shoot so fast, the other teams struggled to keep up with them. They would force the opposing team to play fast on offense as well, trapping opponents even if it meant giving up some easy baskets. Other teams could usually hang in there for a half or so, but eventually, the pace was too much. Westhead coached teams to wear people down, which opened their window to victory.

Our coaches told us to do the same thing in practice to prepare our starters. They said, "If you don't shoot the ball within eight seconds of when we inbound it, you are all coming out, and we will put somebody in who will." We all thought, *What's the catch?* What could possibly be bad about taking the first decent look we got at the basket? Doesn't every player dream of being able to shoot the ball whenever they want? Our coaches also said to give up layups, so the game pace stayed upbeat. "Take the ball out as fast as you can and fire it down court so we can wear them out."

Seriously?

Don't contest layups? This sounded absolutely crazy. It was the first time a coach told me NOT to play defense in my entire life! We began practice with great excitement and ended with great exhaustion. Fortunately, we must have done a decent job preparing the starters as we wound up winning the game 121–96.

Clearly, my role was to get the starters ready to play, and that is pretty much where it stopped. This role continued until late January when we headed to West Lafayette, Indiana, to play Purdue University. The Boilermakers were substantially better than us, and midway through the second half, we were getting pounded. With about a minute and a half left in the game, it finally happened. I heard my name called from the other end of the bench. Coach Ayers yelled for me. He was sending me into the game.

We had been through many lopsided games that season. At Cleveland State, we had so many players foul out that Jerry White and I were the only two players to choose from so we could finish the game with five players on the court. Even though we really needed a post player in the game, Coach Ayers called Jerry's name. He was more physically prepared to play than I was. After that game, I was certain I would never hear my name, but there we were, at the home of the defending Big Ten champions, and I was getting the call!

I was sitting so far away from the coaches that my teammates had to relay my name down the bench so I could hear I was getting called in. Once they got my attention, I sprinted to the scorer's table and took off my warm-up top, waiting until a stoppage of play to enter into the game. As I waited, I peered down at my left arm and shoulder. My skin was a yellowish-brown color from the neckline on my jersey past my shoulder and half way down my arm. I guess one or more of the hits during daily practice had turned into a sizable bruise. It was sore but nothing I hadn't grown accustomed to. To anyone else, I am sure it looked like I had been hit by a truck. I was so embarrassed. Not only did I appear unimposing to our opponent because of my slender build, but I looked like I should skip the game and head to a local urgent care, not into the game.

The horn sounded, and I headed onto the court. The minute plus of playing time was a mere blip on the screen. I felt like I was on the court for about ten seconds. I touched the ball once on a deflection on defense, and that was it.

Scorekeepers didn't chart deflections as official stats, so in the box score I had nothing but zeros all the way across. Our season box score doesn't even show that I played. Nonetheless, I had gotten in a game. I actually played for the Buckeyes. It might have been short and uneventful, but I had played in an official game. When I returned home, my mother and sister told me they had seen the game on TV and were jumping up and down and screaming when I got in. The whole experience brought me a renewed optimism. Who knew where this could take me?

The season was rocky to say the least, but personally, I was on an upswing. I had played against Purdue, and a week later we were playing at Indiana. I had seen impressive Indiana teams play on TV since I started watching games. After seeing them win the title in 1987, I think every kid in the country wanted to learn how to shoot like Steve Alford. Any player growing up during the 1980s, when Indiana won two of their five national titles, would have wanted to play at Assembly Hall regardless of their personal feelings for the team.

Five giant swaying championship banners at one end of the arena reminded anyone who walked into the home of the Hoosiers of their impressive accomplishments. Legendary coach Bobby Knight patrolled their sideline, and their band blared "New Age Girl" by Deadeye Dick. A moment like this one could scarcely be duplicated. This was an intangible gauge of how far I had come as a player. I was a Big Ten player performing on one of the greatest stages in all of college basketball. At that moment, I felt like I could take on the world.

To our dismay, our team didn't play the way I felt. We added another loss to our season that day, and I didn't leave the bench. Still, the experience cemented something in my mind. If I hadn't realized it before, now I definitely knew I loved playing even more than I hated losing. Everywhere we went was a new opportunity to add to my appreciation of the sport. Every game created a new basketball memory. The lore of Assembly Hall rang true that day, and I soaked it all in. No number of losses could take away the enjoyable moments I would gather from this season.

THE WORST OF TIMES

We flew back from Bloomington, Indiana after our game, and I went back to my apartment completely exhausted. Physically and emotionally drained, I was ready for a Sunday with no classes and no practice. My plan was to sleep in for a long, long time. Sound asleep with no alarm clock set, I was so tired I couldn't even hear our phone ring repeatedly throughout the early morning. What I finally did hear was someone pounding on my front door.

Somewhere around 6 a.m., I woke up and ran out to the front room to see why someone was so intent on waking me. I looked through the peephole and saw my friend Chris. I opened the door wondering why on earth he was here so early. As I looked at his face, I immediately knew why. Only one event in my life could bring on such a look. My father had passed away.

Back in August, before basketball tryouts were even a thought in my head, my father had a stroke that left him in an assisted care facility. I didn't take it very well and had a hard time going to visit him. During that first summer of college, we rarely talked. I worked almost fourteen-hour days, and we didn't share anything in common. Even when I did see him, I had no idea what to say.

I had a hard time getting up the courage to go and see him after the stroke. When I finally went to visit, it was even harder than I imagined. He was in pain at times and completely out of sorts. Sometimes he was unsure of who I was. His difficulty was agonizing to witness. Every child wants to forever envision their father as a pillar of strength. From the early days of childhood, Dad is supposed to be Superman. For months after visiting, I struggled with the memory of the experience. I wished more than anything that we had been closer when he was himself. Now my father was gone, and I had no opportunity to go back and change our relationship.

After I collected myself, I called my mom, who said he had passed away on Saturday. She said she hadn't had the heart to tell me because she knew we were playing at Indiana. She explained there wasn't anything that I could have done anyway, so she waited until the next day to tell me.

I immediately made plans to head home. I went back for the services, but I would have to return quickly. I was already overwhelmed with winter quarter classes and the Big Ten season. Missing much of either would make the rest of the school year and the season extremely difficult. I knew that coming to grips with my dad's passing and our lost relationship was going to take a lot longer than a few days, so I went in trying to take things one moment at a time.

I felt numb during the calling hours. The wake was a continuous turnstile of past acquaintances from Canfield shuffling through to pay their respects. I was already emotionally drained from the game, so after this two-day whirlwind, I was completely spent. As the calling hours neared the end, Coach Ayers and Coach Francis walked into the funeral home. They had skipped practice to drive up to Youngstown. I had barely felt like Coach Ayers even knew I was still around. His presence gave me a whole new appreciation for him because he had taken the time to support me in my grief. At practice, he was always intimidating, but this showed me a human side that I really needed to see. His gesture gave me a bit of solace that I needed as the time to head back to Columbus neared. I hoped that my basketball family could help fill the void until I had more time to heal.

I went back to practice the next day. The team went out of their way to make me feel welcome, but I still felt completely removed. At one point, a ball went straight through my hands and hit me square in the face. Normally a play like that would have drawn sneers and jeers for days to come, but the team let that one slide. I was dealing with some serious emotions I hadn't experienced before. Adjusting to the void was going to take a long time.

Following our practice, we left for Evanston, Illinois, to take on Northwestern. I hoped my first trip to Chicago would bring life back into me, but it did not. Any emotion I showed in our game was forced. We came up short against a hapless Wildcat team. In hindsight, I probably shouldn't have traveled to that game. I wasn't myself. I needed more time to reflect, and my brief stint back home wasn't enough. I didn't get an opportunity to grieve properly until the season was over, and even then, it took a lot more time to figure out who I was now that my father was gone and to make peace with our relationship.

Much of the rest of the season was clouded by the loss of my father and more losses by our team. Following the season, we each had a sit-down meeting with Coach Ayers to discuss our futures with the program. When my turn came, I had a lot on my mind. It was hard to think about the future when I still had to work through so much of the past. I thanked him again for coming up to Youngstown in late January. I told him I would like to go home to Canfield for the summer and spend time with my mom and sister, but if it would make a difference in terms of making the team the next season, I would stay to make that happen. I knew playing at Ohio State was a once in a lifetime opportunity, and I wanted to do whatever it took to keep that going.

Coach Ayers responded by saying he believed I knew what I needed to do to improve, and I should go home and spend time with my family. He said I would get an opportunity when I got back in the fall to start out with the team and try out again. I thought this was about all I could ask for, so I thanked him for the opportunity and headed back home to Youngstown for the summer.

Before I left for Youngstown, Coach Francis said he would try to find me a spot on a summer league team in Cleveland or Canton, but neither league worked out. I returned home and began to practice with my old high school team during their summer sessions. Unfortunately, playing against high school talent was not pushing me to grow as a player, so I spent most of my time shooting on my own.

I heard Canfield had a new workout facility, so I headed there to lift weights. One day I started up a conversation with the facility manager on duty. He asked what grade I was in. When I told him I was alumni, he just about blew a gasket. He immediately threw me out wondering why I was in there in the first place. I was shocked. I couldn't believe he was throwing me out. Here I was, a proud alumnus trying to make something of myself, and I was getting tossed out like a complete stranger. There went my weight room for the summer.

As my time in Canfield passed, I was grateful to have the opportunity to heal with my family. Regrettably, the break did not help me grow as a player. I greatly missed the guidance of our coaching staff and the competition of playing against our team each day. Ready or not, summer came to a close, and it was time to head back to Ohio State for my junior year.

CHAPTER 6

Down and Out

On my first day back in Columbus, I headed straight to the basketball coaches' offices and let them know I was back on campus. Their offices were busy and full, as eight new scholarship players were joining the program. After our abysmal season, the coaching staff had worked hard to bring in a whole new squadron of players to erase our failures. While sitting in the offices waiting to talk to our staff, I met Damon Stringer. Damon had played at Cleveland Heights and was Mr. Basketball in Ohio the past season. He headed a star-studded class that was highly ranked entering in as a freshman. I also talked to Coach Roth, who said he would call me as soon as we started workouts. I returned to my apartment and waited to start class and basketball. With two years of academics and a year of basketball under my belt, I was excited about the opportunity to be a leader now that I knew more about how each process worked.

I spent time at the local recreation centers working out and preparing for fall practice. A week or so went by, and I hadn't heard anything. Finally, I decided to call the basketball offices to find out what was going on. An administrative assistant picked up the phone and told me they would have one of the coaches call me back. Later that night, Coach Roth called. The conversation went something like this.

"Hey, Coach Roth. Any more word on when we are planning on getting started with workouts?"

Coach Roth responded, "Well, there has been a change in plans. We decided that we aren't going to have you start out with the team, but you can go through walk-on tryouts if you want."

An awkwardly long pause filled the space. This conversation wasn't going the way I had expected. I had to regroup.

I continued. "Are you planning on keeping anyone on the team from those tryouts?"

"Possibly one or two."

I hung up the phone and began to think. My first reaction was, *Are you kidding me? Why would I have to go through the walk-on tryout? I have already been with the team for a year, and I already proved to be better than the other guys who play on campus. Shouldn't I get at least the benefit of the doubt and start with the team at conditioning? I won't get the support of being involved in the preseason strength program that could help me grow physically. I can't believe they are going to make me wait until the walk-on tryout session. Anybody off the street could come in and try out. Hadn't I earned at least a little more than that?*

After my initial reaction, I started to think in a little more calculated way. According to Coach Roth, one or two players could be taken from the walk-on tryout session. I still loved to play, and I desperately wanted to be on the team. I had gotten a taste of big-time college basketball, and I wanted another. I knew how the entire process worked after going through it, so even if it seemed a bit unfair, I would head back to walk-on tryouts.

I spent the next month lifting weights and playing in Larkins Hall in preparation. On the day of tryouts, I showed up at St. John Arena, and for the second year, the masses did too. I felt encouraged at the end of the session when the coaches called out four names, including mine, to come back. I thought we would return to practice with the team, and in a few weeks, I would have a really good chance of this process shaking out my way. I could run all our drills and all our plays. Heck, I probably would know all of those nuances better than the eight scholarship freshmen! I believed I had a huge advantage.

When the four of us showed up for Monday's practice, Coach Roth met us on one of the ramps leading down to the court. Ironically, it was the ramp that I avoided when I thought I was going to be cut during the past season's tryouts. He said, "Thanks for trying out gentlemen. We wanted to let you know that you were the top four players at the tryout, but we are not going to keep any players at this time. We had all of you stop by so we could let you know we would like you all to stay in shape just in case we need you later this year. If for some reason we get in a situation where we need another player, we will call one of you."

What? Not keeping anyone? Stay in shape?!?!

We didn't even get our shot with the team! I wasn't getting so much as a minute to show how much I remember from last year and how valuable I could be to fill a drill or a scout team position. I felt betrayed and duped. This was not what I was told at the end of last season, nor what I was told when we talked at the beginning of the school year. I was being cut for the first time in my life, and I didn't feel like I got a fair chance.

I guess in the back of my mind, I always knew there was a chance they wouldn't want me. Let's be honest, they had eight new scholarship players that they had to spend their time on. But I really believed because I had accepted my role so well, they would want me to fill it again. After tryouts, I began a stretch that turned into a season-long depression. I wanted so badly to be on the team. I wanted to be around a high level of basketball every day with the hope that I could continue to improve as a player.

As I thought more about it, I really believed my playing in the past season would vanish from existence. No one would believe I played because I didn't have any statistics. I had just one uneventful minute that had been forgotten. I would have to explain my playing at great length to prove it happened. I thought I'd never talk much about my experience because it would sound like I was lying. But more than anything, I just wanted to play. I missed practice and game prep and all that went with it. I had gotten a taste of playing on a Big Ten basketball team and now that was gone.

As the regular season began in early November, I couldn't bear to watch the team play because it was so painful. To think I used to be there and still could be felt like someone cut out my soul. I tried my best to replace the feeling. I played in several men's leagues, even driving over an hour to Marion, Ohio, every Sunday. Frequently I saw how much the year of playing for the Buckeyes had improved my game, yet, playing in a men's league wasn't the same. I wanted more. I felt like I had so much more to give and nowhere to adequately display all I could do.

Struggling to fill my basketball void, I intensified my educational focus. I was an academic junior, and I needed to concentrate on what I planned to do after college. I began to look for internships. If I didn't get an internship that summer, I would have a degree in business the following spring and no job-specific experience to help me gain employment. I needed to step it up and fast. I looked for positions I thought would energize me yet give me the edge I needed after graduation.

Winter quarter was coming to a close. I had a tough final exam coupled with an interview the same day with Nike. I was excited and tense. Sleep became optional while studying for the exam and prepping for the interview. After that all-nighter, I was miserable for at least a week. I decided I would never do that again. Thankfully, I did well enough on the exam to survive the class, and I felt like I nailed the interview. I waited for the results.

A few days later, I got a call from Nike. I didn't get the job. I am not sure if I felt better or worse after they told me I was their second choice. Then the caller informed me I would have got the position if I attended either Texas A&M University or the University of Michigan, but one person from Ohio State fit better. I was beginning to wonder if I was ever going to catch a break again. In a little over a calendar year, I had lost my dad, had been cut from the Ohio State team, and now I had lost a big-time internship, coming in second by a fingernail. I felt as down as I had ever been. I was searching for something, anything, to make me think my hard work would pay off.

I had wanted the position with Nike so badly. Coming so close with nothing to show made me feel worthless. I couldn't help but ask, "Why me?" I was urgently searching for a spark or a sign to get me back on track.

FRESH START

As the stress mounted, I waited impatiently to hear back about one other pending application I had submitted. I had inquired about the Walt Disney World summer internship program in Orlando, Florida. Having completed all the interviews, it was now part of my daily routine to head to the mailbox and wonder each time if this would be the day I would find out the verdict. Finally, as spring was upon us, the day came when a thick, oversized envelope showed up with Walt Disney World in the top left corner. I brought the envelope in from my mailbox and said a brief prayer before I opened it. The letter began something like this:

"Congratulations on being selected to take part in our summer internship program at the Walt Disney World Resort in Orlando, Florida...."

Thank goodness!

I felt as if a tremendous weight had been lifted off my shoulders. I had value again. I was back on track. This was the opportunity I longed to find since I was cut from the team. Finally, my hard work was going to pay off. I would go to Walt Disney World and get a fresh start on life.

Early in June, I packed up my 1990 Ford Mustang and headed for Florida. The '85 Buick Skyhawk was now only a memory. It never would have made a journey of that length. I was basically moving to Orlando for the summer of 1996, so I jammed all my belongings into the hatchback and headed down the coast for a much-needed change of scenery.

The scenery I had viewed growing up was, in a word, limited. There was no doubt in my mind I had grown up in a bubble. My family only left northeastern Ohio a handful of times during my childhood. Other than gyms, hotels, and airports, I hadn't seen much in the year I'd played for the Buckeyes. This was a step toward adulthood that I needed. It was a self-guided adventure. There was a heck of a lot more world outside the Midwest, and it was about time I saw at least a little bit of it.

When I got to Orlando, I moved into an apartment and began training to work on Main Street in the Magic Kingdom. I quickly found we would be working in retail, selling kids clothes, cigars, jewelry, sports apparel, you name it. The shops on Main Street were a mall setup at the entrance and exit of the park. This was where everyone got their souvenirs. The place exuded positivity. The Disney staff had selected "glass half full" people for the internship, and their goal was to improve upon our already positive nature. Our main goal was to seek out those who seemingly weren't having a good time to help them enjoy their experience more. We learned quickly that projecting a solid image, quality posture, and positive energy was contagious. After a few classes and training sessions, we were an integral part of the success of the "Happiest Place on Earth."

LISTEN WITH YOUR HEART

During my first day working on Main Street, I was assigned to a cigar store and smoke shop. I was learning the ropes when a man walked up to me and said something I had heard at least a hundred times since my crazy high school growth spurt.

"Wow, you're really tall. How tall are you?"

I answered with my standard response. "I'm about 6'7"."

His response was standard as well. "Do you play basketball?"

I continued with my now almost rehearsed follow up. "I used to play, but I don't anymore."

The man then asked, "Where did you play?"

I responded, "At Ohio State, for one season."

His interest grew. He continued to inquire. "Do you have any eligibility left?" Almost before the word 'yes' could come out of my mouth, the man was handing me a business card.

I soon found out that the gentleman was the trainer for the men's basketball program at Columbia University. I scribbled out the head coach's name and phone number on the back of the card as he dictated it to me. He said to give him a call if I had any interest in transferring to Columbia to play. I said I would think about it, and he went on his way.

I turned away from our conversation and back to the other interns. They were all stunned. One guy said, "Are you kidding me? You've been working here for five minutes and you get recruited to play basketball at Columbia?" Another asked, "Does this kinda stuff happen to you all the time?" I said, "I don't know. This is my first day."

I have to admit, it felt good to be wanted as a basketball player. I also missed playing competitive college basketball. So, I got up the nerve to call their coach, Armond Hill, to see if this might turn into anything. Here is how the conversation went.

Coach Hill: First off, I am not even allowed to discuss a transfer until you get a release.

Me: A release? They cut me. Doesn't that count as being released?

Coach Hill: It needs to be an official release.

Me: Okay, but please answer a few questions for me so I can gauge how real a possibility this is. First, how many years would I be able to play? I am currently entering into my fourth year at Ohio State.

Coach Hill: Everyone has five years to play four seasons. Since you have already attended three years of college, you would have to sit out a year as a transfer, and then you would have one year of eligibility left to play.

Me: Sit out? I just sat a whole season!

Coach Hill: After you transfer, you'd have your redshirt season, and then you would have one season to play.

Me: Okay, so my second question is, how long will it take me to graduate from Columbia? I am three years deep into pursing a business degree.

Coach Hill: Since you are on the quarters system at OSU and we have semester-long classes at Columbia, a lot of your credits may not transfer. My best estimate is three years of classwork to graduate, depending upon the major you choose.

Me: Okay. One last question. How much does it cost to go to Columbia for a year?

Coach Hill: About $50,000.

Me: Okay. Thank you for the information. I will let you know if I decide to pursue a transfer any further.

After the phone conversation, I began to weigh my options. Smart math said I would basically get to play one year of college basketball and, at the same time, incur $150,000 in debt. This didn't sound like a great financial decision, considering I could be finished with college at OSU in one more year for about a tenth of that price tag—or less. While I was flattered that they would have interest in me playing basketball, and the thought of obtaining an Ivy League education sounded very attractive, it just wasn't a financially realistic option. As unrealistic as it was, the conversation still changed everything. The five-minute discussion I'd had with Coach Hill inspired me to shift my life's momentum.

I firmly believe life is a battle of momentum. After a few weeks, or sometimes even a handful of days of doing something, we can change that momentum. Whether running several miles or making your bed, you form habits from doing a task—or not doing it. I also believe the longer you have done something, the harder it is to change that habit. Positive momentum can carry us through some tough times if we have worked hard to form a quality habit. Every once in a while in life, something inspires us to create a new habit.

The conversation with the trainer from Columbia reminded me of something I had been blocking out for about seven months. I began to reflect on how much I really wanted to play competitive basketball. The talk also made me wonder if I was closer to having another opportunity than I had thought. I decided that while I was working at Disney that summer, I would dedicate all my free time and energy to making the Ohio State team again. With my college days winding down and my love for playing still as strong as ever, this felt like my last shot. I didn't know if making the Buckeyes again was even a real possibility with so many of those freshman scholarship players returning and a hand full of new ones being added as well. Still, if I had learned one thing from the most recent tryouts, it was that giving my maximum effort was all that mattered. I could sleep at night if I knew I gave everything, even if I got cut again. What I couldn't do was live with the thought of *What if I had tried one more time?* That would have eaten me alive. I decided then and there I had to go for it again.

Momentum shift.

I was ready to dedicate myself to basketball for the rest of the summer. I found I had a few items I needed to work through to make that happen. I was taking classes, riding the bus for an hour each way to work, and working full-time plus overtime just to cover the costs of living in Orlando. There wasn't a basketball court for miles, and our apartment complex workout space was mostly for appearances. I would have to get creative with some of these obstacles to make this happen.

EMBRACE THE PROCESS

My plan started with my apartment complex workout facility. There were a few cable machines I used, but I spent most of time adding body weight exercises to increase my strength, including push-ups and sit-ups. We had a pool, so I ran and practiced defensive slides under water to try to improve quickness and speed. Not having a hoop made for another improvisation. We had an indoor racquetball court, so I took my basketball in and worked on dribbling and passing. I asked around and finally located a public court, and drove there, shooting whenever I could. I stayed with this training schedule from June until I left to go back to campus in September. The result was a feeling of empowerment from having rededicated myself to making the team.

The overall Disney experience was exponentially important for me. Having success on my own, far away from home, was a huge growth piece. I became much more comfortable in new places and in uncomfortable situations. I gained confidence in unfamiliar surroundings and talking to anyone. I had always loved the game of basketball, but I learned that summer to love the challenges that come with the process of improving. I applied that growth to my mental toughness as I prepared to return for fall tryouts.

Late in the summer, I had one more Disney moment. I was working some extra hours in a sports memorabilia shop on Main Street. It reminded me a little of the place I worked in high school except this store sold mostly autographs. One of the items for sale was a lithograph picture of several NBA Hall of Fame players including Jerry West, Elgin Baylor, John Havlicek and Dave Cowens. The player I was most excited about was John Havlicek, who was not only a Celtic great and an NBA Hall of Famer, but an Ohio State icon. The autographed lithograph seemed like a fitting memento of the effort I put forth that summer. I carefully packed my purchase in my Mustang hatchback and headed back to Ohio State to start the fall quarter of my senior year.

CHAPTER 7
Try Again

After the long drive back to Columbus, I felt rejuvenated to be back on campus. I had a renewed confidence. I was primed and ready for a senior year filled with maximum effort and considerably more confidence after my summer internship. I was also ready to live with my best effort being the only thing that mattered, whether it was enough to make the team or not.

Soon enough, walk-on tryouts began. I had no contact with the coaching staff before the tryouts. I didn't want to play the mind games of whether or not I thought they needed me or if there was even a spot available. I went to tryouts to show what I had to offer, and I was determined to be at peace with the outcome either way.

For the third year in a row, a multitude of players tried out. And, as I had come to expect based on my prior experiences, the coaches cut the list down to three hopeful young men after a single session. Again, my name was called. We were told to return the next day and start practicing with the team.

Last time I'd heard this, the coaches changed their minds and the walk-on candidates were told to go home before we even laced up our shoes with the team. I had mentally prepared myself for the same thing to happen this year. Fortunately, we did get to practice, but this was different from either of the previous two seasons. The coaches had changed how connected we were with the team from the start. Two years ago, we each got lockers in the varsity locker room, practice gear, and team-issued shoes even during the tryout phase. This time, we weren't so privileged. We wore our own gym clothes, and the coaches laid out reversible practice jerseys to wear each day. They also had us changing in the visitor's locker room at the far end of the arena away from the team.

A year before, I would have thought this was an outrage. I would have viewed this as a slap in the face to someone who was previously a member of the team. I would have felt like an outcast dressing in another locker room as if we had no connection to the actual program. Previously, I would have let this impact my mental focus, and I probably would have played scared throughout tryouts.

Not this time.

After withstanding the past year of heartache and frustration, I was prepared to endure a lot of challenges. The practices went on for several weeks. As I had experienced two years before, there was no communication about our status on the team. I didn't bother asking because I had it in my head to show up and fight until I was told differently. One day, our walk-on number dropped from three to two. I don't know what happened to the third guy, but he never came back. That left a local product named Kwadjo Steele and me as the only two walk-on players.

Kwadjo was a freshman from nearby Westerville North High School. I didn't know him, but I felt like I did because he acted like I had two years earlier. This time, I believed I had a huge advantage knowing drills, plays, and general procedures of practice. Kwadjo looked like a fish out of water at times as practices developed. He frequently appeared nervous, as anyone in his position would. This made me feel even better about my growth because I wasn't that player anymore. I had grown into someone with more resiliency. Still, I kept my defenses up because the coaches didn't keep anyone the previous year.

One day after practice, Kwadjo and I were changing in the visitors' locker room. We hadn't really talked before. We both had been focused on the business of trying out. I noticed he seemed to be extra worried. I couldn't help but think that must have been how I looked throughout my entire first experience of trying out. I stopped changing for a moment and said, "Look, don't worry. Relax and play. They need us. Just play your game, and everything is going to work out."

Kwadjo responded with only a nod, but I could see my comment had an effect on him by the way his demeanor immediately changed. Those were the words I'd needed my first time around, but no one had ever said them to me. It was something, anything, that would provide a little comfort in a very stressful setting. I think I said those words as much for myself as I did for him. I wanted very much to believe there was real hope for us to make the team.

The crazy part was I didn't really know if what I said had any truth to it. It was my gut feeling based on the number of guys who were healthy and practicing. Maybe I was trying to boost my own confidence as we continued to push through preseason practices. Regardless, I tried to play with a quiet poise and edge. I thought to myself, *What can you do to me that hasn't already been done? I've already been cut once. I've already experienced one gut-wrenching tryout where no one ever told me if I had made the team, and another where*

*the coaches changed their thoughts about walk-ons daily.
How could this be any worse? Don't give me practice gear?
Fine. Put me in the visitors' locker room? Go for it. I can
take whatever you dish out. I already have multiple layers
of basketball scar tissue built up around my heart. What's a
little more going to hurt?*

That doesn't mean I still didn't have my moments of
concern. Partway through the preseason, I started not feeling
well. I was excessively fatigued, even beyond what our
practices normally caused, and decided I should go to the
clinic on campus to see if they could help me. They told me I
might have walking pneumonia. Obviously, this brought on
immediate and intense concern.

I thought if I missed practice, much less several practices,
due to illness, I would get cut for sure. As I tried to read the
tea leaves, I knew John Lumpkin was still to be added to the
team after the football bowl game, so maybe they had gotten
almost all of what they needed from me by now. I couldn't
make their decision easy by sitting out a week of practice.
Tired and concerned, I walked back to my apartment
searching for answers. I was starting to feel overwhelmed.

The streets were full of students hurrying between
classes. Then a steady rain started falling, adding even
more urgency to our rush. I too was trying my best to
hustle through the crowd. I already felt weak, and I didn't
have any desire to add to my discomfort by getting soaked
in cold late-October rain. I had only a few hours before
practice, and I had a list of things to get done prior to
heading over to St. John Arena.

I was in the middle of Neil Avenue about twenty yards
from the path that leads past Mirror Lake when my
backpack suddenly broke open like a piñata at a four-year-
old's birthday party. When I say the bag broke open, I mean

it basically exploded. It wasn't zipped all the way to the top, and the weight of my folders and books caused it to unzip by itself at lightning speed. The contents now dotted the street like confetti as students frantically scurried through the shower.

For a moment, I had a pity party for myself. I knelt down and looked around at the metaphor of the situation. My life felt a lot like the backpack that was now in pieces. I was unsure if I would make the team, stressed out over classwork that needed to be completed, and sick to top it all off. Now my academic life was strewn all over Neil Avenue and I was getting soaked.

Suddenly, another student stopped and began to selflessly help me pick up all the pieces, literally and figuratively. As the young lady helped me grab all my things before they got ruined, my mood instantly improved. It is amazing what a small act of kindness can do. This moment, however minor and pedestrian, has stuck with me to this day. To think that someone who had no connection to me would stop in the middle of a torrential downpour of freezing rain to aid a complete stranger was, in a word, uplifting. I thanked her and while I never saw her again, she left me with renewed energy and inspiration. That was the spark I needed. It immediately shifted my momentum back to positive energy.

I went to my apartment, got some rest, and ignored the classwork I needed to accomplish for the moment. I went to practice with a clear head and revitalized spirit. I had improved focus by connecting with the task at hand. I worked hard to try to make it through one event at a time and not become overwhelmed with the big picture. That focus helped me endure the next several weeks of practice and classes. I am sure my play was average at best, but my renewed approach was somehow enough to keep me from getting sent home. Gradually my health and my outlook began to improve.

I kept pushing forward with a little more belief every day. Having now had some time to process all of the events that had happened over the past year, I had a new perspective. I was beginning to think that getting cut the year before was possibly the best thing that could have happened to me. I had never been cut before that season in anything I had done. It wasn't because I was so great at everything. The reason was if there was a chance that I might lose out or get cut, I walked away so as not to look inferior. I had now experienced what it was like to give my best and have it not be enough. On the surface, failure doesn't come off as a good thing. No one likes to look bad or be considered inferior by their peers. But in truth, the only way to improve in life is to consistently challenge yourself to risk failure. If you don't find that failure point, then you can't grow. You will consistently remain the same old player you were in the past. If you don't give something a try at all and walk away, you will always wonder if you were good enough. You will spend the rest of your life saying, "Maybe I could have done it if I'd just tried."

That wasn't good enough for me anymore. I found myself considerably more fulfilled after sticking my neck out there and finding what my best was. This is a clichéd statement, but I agree that the only true failure is not trying. Because I had gotten cut my second time around, I found it easy to rest my head on my pillow every night. As long as I knew I had done everything I could to try to make it happen, I could sleep well.

This calm and belief helped me tremendously during that tryout period. No longer did I take anything that our coaches said personally. They could be a blunt and abrasive group at times, but that was to get us ready to play elite basketball. I could handle that kind of feedback much better because I had been cut the year before. Now I needed to keep grinding through mentally as we navigated week after week of long and physically demanding preseason practices.

PRESEASON GRIND

Practices were tough, especially when we went through double sessions each day in the preseason. At one point or another, we all daydreamed we were somewhere else. At minimum, we wished our bodies could get a reprieve. To give an idea of how badly some of us needed rest, consider what Sean Tucker was willing to do to get out of practicing.

Sean was a freshman from Mansfield, Ohio, who went to Ohio State by way of a year in prep school at Maine Central Institute. He was a strong, bruising forward with tremendous aggression. One day during the second of two practices, we took a quick break following an intense rebounding drill. The coaches told us to split up between all the baskets to shoot free throws and then get a drink. Tuck, as we called him, and I were at the same hoop. As we lined up to shoot, Tuck said to me, "Man, I'm done. Coach turns his head, I'm outta here!"

I didn't know Sean really well at that point, but I already pegged him to be a guy who would probably say some bold things without much intention of following through. I shrugged it off as something any of us would have said out of pure exhaustion. We shot our free throws, got our water, and returned to practice. I didn't think any more of his statement.

When the coaching staff blew their whistles for us to come back, Coach Roth had pulled together the second team huddle, which Tuck and I were a part of during each practice session. Coach Roth looked around and didn't see Tuck. With annoyed curiosity, he asked everyone, "Where's Tuck?"

I thought, *No way!?! Did he really leave? No. He must be using the restroom. There is no way he would try to sneak out … would he?* I didn't dare say anything. Coach Roth followed by hollering, "Jerry (Francis), go find him!"

As Coach Francis described later when telling the story, he went in the locker room and looked under the bathroom stalls. He saw nothing. He went to Tuck's locker and saw his practice gear was already hung up. Then he ran outside and headed in the direction of Morrell Tower, where the freshman players lived. When he didn't see Tuck walking toward the tower, he began to head back to practice, wondering where in the world he could have gone.

Coach Francis then looked back toward the arena. Tuck, who was wearing his bright purple corduroy overalls that day, was hiding behind some bushes right outside St. John Arena. His attire was pretty much the complete opposite of wearing camouflage. What made the situation even more humorous was that the bushes had already lost their leaves, so hiding behind the sticks that remained was an utterly hopeless strategy. Coach Francis immediately dragged Tuck back in and had him put his sweaty practice gear back on so he could finish the session along with some extra conditioning.

Now back to our tryout.

Kwadjo and I kept showing up for practice and, similar to my experience from two years before, no one updated us on whether we had made the team. Pictures had been taken prior to the walk-on tryout, so this wouldn't have helped us find out our statuses either. We finally got moved over to the regular locker room a handful of days before the start of the regular season. When this happened, the coaches told us to get team-issued practice gear and sent us down to the equipment manager to get squared away.

The number twenty-three jersey that I had worn my first time around was now worn by Jason Singleton, who had come in as one of those eight highly touted freshmen now entering their sophomore campaigns. I didn't mind that he was wearing it. When he came in, I wasn't even on the team, so he didn't owe me anything. I was ready for a fresh start anyway because I felt like a different player. When the equipment manager asked me what number I wanted, I almost fainted. I wasn't used to getting to choose what happened during this process. That was refreshing. I selected number forty-four and set off on a new mission. I wanted to be someone our coaches felt needed to be on the court to help us win. Before that could happen, I had to get full confirmation I was on the team, like actually being in uniform at a game.

SECOND SEASON

Our first game was November twenty-third at South Florida. I was excited to head back to the "Sunshine State" because I had just spent the summer there committing myself to making the team. I thought it would be poetic to restart my career in the place where I had rededicated myself to the game. It seemed to fit in the storyline perfectly.

Two days before the trip, Coach Roth called Kwadjo and me into the coaches' offices. I am not sure why he always ended up being the coach who was the bearer of the bad news. I can't imagine he would have wanted to be that guy all the time. He said we wouldn't be traveling with the team to South Florida because they were flying commercial, and the tickets were bought before we were in the plan. All the seats were accounted for and set in stone.

I was deeply disappointed because the last time I'd made it this far, I got to travel and be in uniform for all the games. There went my perfect storybook return to glory. I thought about it for a little while and decided I could live with the explanation on this one. If they had made the arrangements prior to walk-on tryouts, how could I not? They had no way to foresee this. I accepted the clarification and moved forward.

The next day after practice, I had an interesting discussion with one of our senior student managers. He was talking about how he didn't want to go to our road game against South Florida because it was going to cause him to miss the Ohio State–Michigan football game. He had great seats for the game because he was a senior, and he didn't want to miss out. He told the coaching staff he had a really important exam that he couldn't reschedule, and it was going to cause him to miss the team flight (which was true). He hoped this would cement his chance to see the rivalry in the horseshoe.

My initial thought was, *Wow, are you really trying that hard to miss our game in Florida?* Here I was desperately wanting to do the exact opposite. I would have done just about anything to get on that flight. I was thinking to myself, *Shoot, I'll take your spot on the plane!* Then he told me the really frustrating part of the story.

He said Coach Roth had told him that it was no problem to get him another flight for the next morning. So, to his disappointment, he could still go to our early season road game. What that also meant was our coaches had the power to change the airline tickets. Translation, it appeared that Kwadjo and I weren't important enough to bring along.

To say I felt betrayed is an understatement. I thought, *Seriously? Coach Roth told me they couldn't get us tickets, yet they were able to get a student manager a next-day flight with almost no notice?* It was hard to feel like we mattered if they were working harder to bring non-players to the game than to bring Kwadjo and me. I felt like if the situation were different, and they really needed a player, they would have found a way to get him to the game.

I can't describe how weird I felt watching that South Florida game on television at home in Columbus. I was healthy enough to play, yet I was watching the game on TV like anyone else. Seeing the game with my friends felt more like the previous season when I was cut from the team. I cheered for us to win, but large parts of me selfishly wanted the game to be over so I could get back to feeling like I was part of the program.

The South Florida game ended with a close defeat. The team, including Kwadjo and me, returned to practices in preparation for a stretch of home games. The team and my psyche bounced back in the weeks that followed. We won our next five games, all at home, and I was in uniform for all of them. I even got several moments of playing time in a couple of the games. Each time was a minute or less, and I had no stats to report, but to me this was still monumental progress. This was proof I was on the team. My playing was much earlier in this season than during my previous stint, and we seemed to be a better team overall. This was an encouraging sign for both the team and me. Things looked to be on a gradual upswing.

GRIN AND BEAR IT

During my second season of play, I was constantly matched up with either Shaun Stonerook, a highly touted sophomore who played for a state championship team at Westerville North High School, or Jason Singleton. Singleton was a high school phenom from Aquinas High School in Detroit, Michigan, who was quite possibly the most athletic player in all of college basketball by the time he graduated. Both were very mobile, athletic forwards who were tough to guard, but they helped me improve daily. One day in practice I was guarding Jason in the corner and he began to slash toward the basket. He drove baseline toward the hoop and went up with every intention of dunking the ball on anyone who got in his way. I was pretty savvy on this particular play and timed up my block attempt well. When I touched the ball with my left hand, Jason lifted his elbow in an attempt to create some space and avert the block. As a result, I took a blow straight to the mouth. His elbow made direct contact with my front tooth and broke it off clean in the middle. Somehow, I partially blocked the shot, caught the tooth in my other hand and then tossed it aside while I kept playing.

I am not sure if Coach Ayers saw exactly what happened during the play. When he finally did see me without a front tooth, he took the opportunity to preach about wearing a mouth guard during practice. I respected his view on wearing a mouth piece, but I felt like I couldn't breathe or talk while playing or running with one, so I never wore it. Now I would pay the price in the dentist's chair.

The next day, I headed to the OSU College of Dentistry to get fixed up. First, they made me a temporary tooth to wear until they could make a veneer that matched the rest of my teeth. Once that was finished, they called me back in to put on the new veneer permanently. That's when things got really crazy.

First, the hygienist attempted to remove the temporary veneer, which was easier said than done. They couldn't get it loose from the tooth, so when they finally pried it off, the veneer broke off more of the tooth. The portion that remained needed a root canal. They continued the process with what seemed like half of the university watching. Apparently when you had a procedure done at the OSU College of Dentistry, students at different stages of their educational progression looked on to fulfill class requirements. I was okay with others watching, although I felt like it was taking forever. The small army of rotating students seemed to be growing as the hours passed.

Suddenly, things came to a stop. It felt like they had been probing for a while, and that wasn't a good feeling. The dental student working on my tooth went to get one of the professors. Then that professor got another. They moved me to an oral surgery room and continued to probe inside my tooth, also not good. I felt like they were looking for something.

At some point during the process, the student had broken off one of the rasps they use to gut the tooth during the root canal. This minutely sized piece of file was stuck way up inside my tooth, and they had to fish it out. Again, no part of this was good. Finally, after what felt like an eternity, the broken piece was removed and the root canal was finished. They decided to send me home because I had been there for more than four hours. That was a lot longer than I had expected, and it was dinner time. I'm sure we all needed a break. After receiving instructions on how to take my pain medications, it was time to call it a day. I would have to live with half a front tooth until they could schedule the rest of the procedure for later on that week.

I went home and got something to eat, took my pain meds, and began to clean up. While I was moving some laundry from the washer to the dryer, I started to feel extremely tired. This feeling wasn't that uncommon with the amount of physical activity I exerted during daily practices, but this exhaustion felt even more overwhelming than usual. I thought I was going to fall asleep while actively switching laundry. That wasn't normal.

I quickly thought back through what I had done since returning from the dentist. Then I looked back at my pain meds. The dentist had said to take either three ibuprofen tablets or one hydrocodone pill for the pain. Then it hit me. Had I taken three hydrocodone pills by accident? I must have! That was the only explanation for feeling like I was going to pass out standing up. I was so groggy from the four hours of dental work and the pain meds I had already taken that I had royally messed up the amount I was supposed to take when I got home!

I immediately called the emergency number our trainer, Mike Bordner, had given us in case we ever needed help with something injury-related. I dialed in a panic. I was really glad he answered. The conversation went something like this.

Mike Bordner: Hello?

Me: Hey, Bords. I am a little worried over here. I went in to get my tooth fixed and long story short, I accidentally took three hydrocodone pills for the pain instead of three ibuprofen tablets. Should I make myself throw up?

Mike Bordner: No, you don't need to do that. Just don't operate any heavy machinery or drive anywhere. Head to bed, and you'll be fine. You're going to sleep for a good while, but you're going to be fine.

So, I headed off to bed, and Bords was right. I slept for a good while. I had one of the deepest, soundest sleeps I have ever had. I woke up fourteen hours later. Never before or since have I slept that long a stint. I felt very well-rested and headed out for the day, still having only half of a front tooth.

What was on the agenda for that day? Well, I had agreed weeks before to go to a middle school that was having a family fun night as a fundraiser. I was to have my own booth, sign autographs and talk with the people who stopped by about my Ohio State basketball experience. I was excited about being asked to do it. It made me feel like sort of a celebrity and certainly like a valued member of the team. Now, instead, I had replaced that excitement with anxiety because I was attending this event with only half of a front tooth.

And that was only half my worry.

The other concern was that earlier in the week I dove for a loose ball while playing and had gotten kicked in the head. At the time, I hadn't thought about the play other than I was the first guy on the floor, and I got the loose ball for my team. Now the kick had turned into a black eye that was all sorts of purple, yellow, black, and green colors. Add in a broken tooth, and I looked like a train wreck. As parents and students approached me for autographs, they gave me a look as if to ask, "Did this guy get mugged in the parking lot?"

A few days later, I went back to the dentist to get my veneer. In all, I logged four separate visits and approximately sixteen hours in the dental chair to complete the procedure, but I never missed so much as a play of practice. I tried diligently to follow the Jerry West quote, "You can't get much done in life if you only work on the days when you feel good." Even with the tooth incident, I am proud to say (and also very lucky) that I never missed a practice while playing at Ohio State.

LEARNING CURVE

Over the holiday break, we had the chance to take an extended road trip that had us headed all the way to

California. This would be my first trip to the West Coast. We played The University of Southern California and San Diego State. Both teams were solid, so we hoped for a good showing. Unfortunately, we didn't have one. We lost both games. Our flight back to Columbus felt like a funeral. I could tell Coach Ayers expected at least a split of the two games, and we couldn't pull off a single win.

Next, we headed to Cleveland for the Gatorade Shootout, where we played the defending national champions, the University of Kentucky. Their roster included five future first round NBA draft picks, including senior shooting guard Derek Anderson, who was such an incredible talent that even though he missed most of the rest of the season from tearing his ACL after our game, he still was picked by the Cleveland Cavaliers thirteenth overall. I found it ironic that we played his team because he was one of the players whose exit gave me a chance to make the team my first time around.

We competed throughout the game, but eventually Kentucky pulled away. For most, the locker room was filled with frustration following the game. For a couple of immature players, it was a time for laughter. To the chagrin of everyone who was doing the right things, Coach Ayers caught those players clowning around, and that put us in a really bad spot. We drove back to Columbus and practiced late into the night as soon as we got home. Overall, we were now 5–4 and had lost to every high-quality team we played in the non-conference. Now the Big Ten was starting, so games weren't getting any easier.

We opened up Big Ten play at Michigan. We came out ready to compete and shocked everyone with a win. Following the game, the locker room was bedlam. It was a tiny space, and our team consumed the room, jumping up and down until we couldn't jump anymore. We could see that Coach Ayers was proud of us. We had endured a season and a half of him being disappointed with so many outcomes. It was uplifting to see him excited along with the rest of the team. Winning a road game against our traditional rival Michigan was a win we needed. When we returned to St. John Arena, people were lined up to greet us, congratulating us on our efforts. That joyful welcome reminded all of us why we had started playing the game in the first place.

After splitting a pair of games against Illinois and Penn State, we had a 2–1 Big Ten record. That put us right in the mix near the top of the league. We were headed to Michigan State (MSU) to play an up and coming Spartan team. They had Mateen Cleaves, Morris Peterson, and A. J. Granger, who were some of the rising stars that season not only in the Big Ten, but around the country.

Our team could boast of a handful of rising stars as well. The bulk of those eight scholarship freshman, now sophomores, started to show why they were included in one of the top recruiting classes in the country. Our 2–1 start in league play had people talking about us. I even read an article reporting that the winner of our game at MSU looked to be the team of the future in our league.

The Breslin Center in East Lansing was energized, and the game was close. We fought hard, but ended up on the short end, 69–66. That started a four-game skid that was undoubtedly enhanced by the pain of that loss. Morale got so low that we lost by thirty-one points to lowly Northwestern. Our team energy appeared to be about as bad as it could be, and mine was taking a hit too. Before one game during that stretch, one of the other players on our team was tired of waiting to get his ankles taped. When it was my turn, he decided to take his impatience out on me. He clamored, "Why do you even get taped for games? You're not going to play!"

Sadly, the scores showed he was basically right. While I thought I was doing a lot in practice to help get the team ready to play, that wasn't translating into playing time for me or victories for us. I was busting my tail in hopes of improving enough to get on the floor, but our coaching staff had to invest in the younger scholarship players they were banking on to turn the program around. It wasn't the first time I had been torn down by comments like this, but it still hurt. I wasn't bulletproof. I had to do some real soul searching to stay positive. It seemed we had hit rock bottom.

...Or had we?

NEXT MAN UP

When we went back to practice Monday, we found out that Sean Tucker had hurt his knee. An MRI revealed he had a partial tear from years before that needed surgery. He was out for the season. This wasn't the only new concern we had. We also learned that week that Jermaine Tate, our starting center and impressive force in the paint, was having some heart irregularities and was also finished for the year.

So, we were down two post players with mighty Indiana coming to town. On the day of the game, I went to change for our pregame shootaround. I walked past the coaches' locker room when Coach Ayers stopped me. He was getting ready for shootaround himself. The whole conversation was kind of humorous because he never stopped changing while he was talking. In fact, I'm not sure he ever actually looked up at me. Here is how the conversation went.

Coach Ayers: "Eric, with all that has happened this week, we are going to need you tonight. You're ready. You've been working hard, and I know you can give us some good minutes off the bench."

Me: "Okay."

And that was that. I kept walking. Immediately, my nerves went berserk. The shootaround was a blur. At pregame meals, I usually ate like a king. I had recognized that I wasn't going to see the court for more than a couple minutes, so I didn't worry about filling up before the game. If I were going to play, it would be the end of the game, which was about six hours after the pregame meal. Who wouldn't make sure they had a good meal in my position, right?

Now, I was surely in the game, and I was playing what I used to call "real minutes" or minutes where the game was yet to be decided. In my entire career, minus less than a handful of games as a senior in high school, I had never known prior to the game if I would be involved in meaningful minutes. My stomach was in a knot. I could barely force food down. This was a big opportunity, and I didn't want to mess it up.

My big opportunity came late in the first half, and it was a quick couple of possessions that were fairly uneventful. The memorable highlight was sprinting back defensively and having Neil Reed make a savvy play by trying to slow his dribble in front of me so I would run over him, thus helping him get to the free throw line. Fortunately, I stopped on a dime to avoid him.

Not more than a minute or two later I was back out. I didn't participate in plays of importance, but I didn't make any errors that sabotaged the game either. A whole different feeling came over me. I had played when the game was in doubt. It gave me new life. Even though I hadn't scored, rebounded, or blocked anything, I felt like I mattered and contributed to the team's success. And what made the experience even better was that we won. I might not have had any stats, but I had been in the mix in a huge upset.

After a brief celebration with our coaches, I sat back for a minute in the locker room to digest our accomplishment. I had finally gotten the opportunity to play meaningful minutes in an important game against a good team, an NCAA tournament team that would end up 22–11 that season. What an extremely rewarding feeling to have overcome all the injuries and odds to help pull out a win.

What I hadn't realized was that the player on our team who had given me a hard time about getting taped up for games had not played that night. When we unlaced our shoes and headed for the showers, another player who had overheard the previous comment about not playing realized the irony. He asked him, "So why did you bother to get taped for the game?" I couldn't help but smile inside a little. I had been bullied by comments like that for so many years that it was nice to have someone stick up for me.

IN THE BOOKS

After beating Indiana, a well-respected perennial power with our skeleton crew of a team, we had another formidable opponent coming to town in Wisconsin. They were 11–6 at the time. We didn't have much turn-around time either. We started to prep for a quality Badger team who appeared poised for a run in the NCAA tournament. I'm not sure anyone thought we could pull off back-to-back success stories, but we were like an injured animal running on adrenaline. We searched for a little more juice to keep our momentum going.

A packed crowd at St. John Arena saw our team scrap to another victory. For me, the magic came in the waning moments of the contest. I had played a few fleeting possessions during the game, and I didn't play particularly well. During the last few minutes, I was beat on a drive to the basket on defense that cost us a score. Then I was fouled and missed the front end of a one-and-one in my first chance to score as a Buckeye. Next, I missed a box out on defense that lead to more Wisconsin points. I played poorly and suddenly doubted myself a lot.

On the next offensive possession, I got fouled again and went back to the free throw line. I missed the first of two free throws. I was yet to do anything positive since I entered the game and was starting to wonder what else could go wrong. Then I caught a glimpse of someone in the stands.

During my career, I was pretty good at tuning out the crowd. I'd look up into the stands at our players' family and friends' section long enough to see that my mother and sister had made it down to the game from Youngstown. After that, I never looked up again. I was always locked into what was going on during the game to be mentally ready if my number was called. When I played in a game, there was no time for anything other than the task at hand. At that moment, I just wanted to find a way to get the ball to go in the basket.

One time.

On this night, when I was ultimately frustrated and lacked confidence, something made me look off into the crowd between free throw attempts. By chance, I made out a familiar face. It was my old youth coach, Chris Calpin, in the stands. I had recently run into him in the City Center Mall and learned he lived in Columbus. He said he was working in planning and engineering for the City of Columbus and lived near Ohio State. I told him I had made the Buckeyes team, and he said he would try to come by for a game sometime.

When I saw him, I had a momentary life flashback. I thought back to fourth grade and how Chris taught us how to shoot. I thought about being bullied in middle school and how energized I was when Chris came to help our team. The memories made me think about all the work and hardship I had gone through from a basketball standpoint to get here. That immediately changed my demeanor. I went from thinking, *What could possibly go wrong next?* and *Please don't miss this free throw* to, *I deserve this free throw,* and *I am cashing in on this opportunity.*

I stepped to the line and nailed the second free throw for the first point of my Ohio State career. It felt like someone took a cap off the rim and a weight off my shoulders at the same time. I finally scored a point for the Buckeyes, and Chris Calpin, my very first coach, was in attendance. Add to the excitement that we had won again, and we were back to .500 on the season. Maybe we still had a little gas in the tank. Maybe we could put together a miracle playoff run.

RUNNING ON EMPTY

After our win against Wisconsin, we were the *Sporting News* National Team of the Week. We had overcome two season-ending injuries with Jermaine and Sean. What was next on our schedule? We had to head to Purdue and then to Indiana, whom we had just beaten at home. Neither of those road games in Indiana would be easy. Could our good fortune continue for another week of Big Ten games?

In a word, no.

Our momentum as a team and my individual success had run out. In fact, I never saw the court again that season. We lost both of those games by double digits, which sent us to nine losses compared to seven wins and to the brink of destruction. A win against a hapless Northwestern squad gave us a glimmer of hope, but we couldn't seem to completely seal the deal. Our team chemistry wasn't cohesive, and we were undermanned and running out of the magic we found during that one special week at the end of January.

We followed up with losses to Minnesota and Iowa that put us at 10–13 on the year. Still, if we could find a way to get hot again, there were enough games left for us to salvage a winning record and earn a bid to the NIT. We tried to muster another charge. Fighting to stay alive for the postseason, we put up another strong performance against Michigan State but lost at home by a basket. This was a crushing defeat for our team. We seemed so close in potential to that Michigan State squad, yet we couldn't get over the hump against them. While we might not have been that far from each other, they were building team chemistry, and we seemed to be spiraling out of control.

Next, we headed for Penn State, a team we had soundly beaten earlier in the year. We played as if we were dead on our feet in the first half. We were devoid of emotion knowing that after the MSU loss, our chances at making the postseason were a memory.

After a handful of desperate speeches by Coach Ayers, we scrambled back to within two points and had a chance to win in the last minute of regulation. Coach Ayers frantically drew up a last second play during our final time out, and we got a decent look at the basket, but our game winning shot attempt fell short. We went home with yet another loss. We followed our un-Happy Valley heartbreaker with another uninspired performance against the Illini, losing by seven at their place. That left us with only one more chance to salvage a victory and only one more opportunity to put a positive stamp on the 1996–1997 season.

Senior Night was a home contest against Michigan, and while I was a senior academically, no one approached me to discuss any pomp and circumstance about the evening. I had no idea whether I would get a chance the next year, but I did know I wanted to keep playing. I had one more year of eligibility, and I wanted to use it. But that was something to worry about another day. Right now, we were preparing to play our rival. We had beaten Michigan way back at the beginning of January when the season still looked bright. Now our team was broken and battered and urgently trying to salvage any good feeling we could before the offseason was upon us.

Still, there couldn't have been a better game to have left. Playing Michigan always had meaning. We still had the opportunity to beat our rival and sweep them for the first time in years. Networks were also saying a loss would cost Michigan the chance to get in the NCAA tournament. I could see why the football program has played Michigan at the end of the season for the better part of a century. We'd all heard die-hard Buckeye fans say they would rather go winless and beat Michigan than do the opposite. This was our opportunity to make those fans a lot happier with our season. In the end, we had plenty to play for with this match up. We were playing our rival on senior night with the chance to snatch the ultimate prize away from them. This should be enough motivation for any team to put forth their best effort.

And we did just that. For a team that was six games under .500, we fought like crazy. This was our NCAA tournament. We had scratched and clawed our way to a six-point lead with thirty seconds left in the game. The bench felt alive. We could feel a second victory against the "team up North" within our grasp.

And then it happened.

Whatever could go wrong in the last thirty seconds did. We let Michigan come all the way back and send the game into overtime. We then played overtime as if the game had ended in regulation.

Michigan 86–Ohio State 81.

This loss not only stung in the moment, but it summed up our entire season. We were a talented team. We were capable of 17–10 or better. We were probably good enough to challenge for an NCAA tournament spot if only we could have found a flow as a unit. We had shown Michigan that potential for thirty-nine and a half minutes, but we couldn't generate enough chemistry or belief to finish the job. Our season was over with a record of 10–17. Anyone wearing scarlet and gray could feel changes were coming in the men's basketball program. I just hoped those changes didn't send me and my bags packing.

CHAPTER 8
Who's Your Coach?

ood news for me, I wasn't the first person packing my bags. Coach Ayers was the one heading for the exits. Bad news, he was the guy who had given me the opportunity to be part of the program. With all the struggles we had endured, I still owed him a tremendous amount of thanks. He was the one person who gave a guy with virtually no experience a chance to be part of a major Division I program. So, without Coach Ayers at the helm, I didn't know if I had a future with the team.

I began to ponder my next step. I had one year of eligibility left, and I still needed a handful of classes to qualify for graduation with only spring quarter left in my academic senior year. The NCAA didn't have one-year graduate transfers back then. This left me with either finishing up in the summer or sticking it out until next fall and maybe giving it one more go with a new staff. The latter option would bring no guarantees. I decided to do some soul searching again. What better place to do it than at the Final Four?

The Final Four was scheduled to be played in Indianapolis early in the spring. That meant it was going to be only three hours from our campus in Columbus. One of our managers,

Mark Neustadt, and I had talked about how much we wanted to attend the Final Four. Much like I had in high school when I had gone to the state tournament, I wanted to go see what it was like to achieve the ultimate success at the collegiate level. I wanted to see in person how good those teams really were.

On a cold day in late March, Mark and I drove to Indy, where plenty of buzz swirled around the Final Four games. Kentucky was going for back-to-back titles, and they were joined by a dominant Minnesota team lead by Bobby Jackson, Sam Jacobson, John Thomas and Quincy Lewis. All four were eventually NBA draft picks. We had played both of those teams during the regular season, making the Final Four even more interesting to Mark and me. Also joining the Wildcats and Gophers were the North Carolina Tar Heels, who were led by Hall of Fame Head Coach Dean Smith. No one knew at the time, but he would retire after that season. Those in attendance watched him coach his last game when they played an upstart Arizona team in their Final Four game.

Tickets were expensive what with North Carolina and Kentucky, two blue blood basketball programs being in attendance. Since Minnesota was within driving distance, prices rose steadily as game time neared. I paid $225 to go to all three games, a sizable amount at the time. The expense ended up being well worth it to watch a Miles Simon-led Arizona team become the first school ever to beat three number one seeds on their way to winning the title.

You couldn't have asked for a more exciting tournament, what with the championship game going into overtime, but all I could think about on the drive back to Columbus was the interaction I'd had with fans on the street prior to the game. I was wearing my Ohio State letterman's jacket with pride as we walked around the frigid streets of Indianapolis.

I hadn't realized what a mistake that was until we hit the pavement. As we walked around, I was stopped repeatedly by people who wanted to know who our next coach was going to be. Of course, I had no idea. I was a forgotten walk-on with no insider information. The questions got pretty old after about twenty minutes of saying, "I have no idea who we will hire." The frequent interactions became a continual reminder that I didn't know what my basketball future was either.

UNEXPECTED HIRE

After Arizona was crowned NCAA champion for the first time, I felt like my second stint with the Buckeyes had some closure. The Arizona win had rejuvenated me as a player. The way our season had ended made feeling defeated easy, but this experience showed me what was possible. Seeing two of the teams we played that season playing for the ultimate prize in Indianapolis made basketball glory feel closer to reality than at first glance. I made up my mind that I would stick around another year to try to play again and capture the magic that was college basketball. It was only a two-quarter commitment in the grand scheme of life, and I didn't have a concrete post-graduation plan anyway. It was an easy call. I wanted more basketball.

Still, I had lots of work ahead, and a lot of doubt about what the foreseeable future held. April of my senior year had begun, and I needed to improve my game. I was committed to getting bigger, stronger, and more skilled in an effort to impress our new coach, so he'd keep me around.

Hold on. Who was our new coach?

It had been almost a month since Coach Ayers was fired. We had regularly scheduled lifting and open gyms throughout that stretch without a coaching staff. I had been to the Final Four and back, and we still didn't have a leader. It felt like an eternity of waiting to know who would be the next Buckeyes head coach.

Exactly one week after the national championship game, I was walking in to open gym and saw countless trucks from local television stations outside of St. John Arena. Some big news was about to be released. I went into the locker room and sat down to change for open gym. One of the reporters came over and sat next to me. He was the brother of a friend. He frequently would say hello to me, and in response I would always ask him, "Hey, you need any quotes from me today?" He always smiled and said. "No thanks." As usual, he didn't need any sound bites, but he did have news for me.

"Have you heard who they hired?" he asked.

"No. Who is it?"

"Jim O'Brien, from Boston College."

I didn't quite know how to react. The fact that we as a team hadn't found out who the new coach was prior to the media had caught me off guard. Second, the selection was pretty much out of left field for me. I wasn't expecting an East Coast coach to be hired. Then I started to think back through what I remembered about Boston College from the past few seasons. I vividly recalled that they had upset North Carolina, a number one seed a year or so earlier on their way to the Sweet Sixteen. Immediately I began to think that this coach could take talent to their maximum level. He might not have been the flashy name I thought Ohio State would get, but I was intrigued with the hire. Here was an overachieving coach who might appreciate the scrappy player I was trying to be.

The real question was whether he would even bother to get to know me or begin to bring in transfers left and right.

He quickly brought in Scoonie Penn, an all-Big East point guard whom he had originally recruited to Boston College. Scoonie decided to follow O'Brien when he left. Rumors circulated that more transfers could be on the way, but I couldn't worry about that. I had to worry about the work I had to do to even have a chance to be around.

Immediately I made an effort to get to know our new coaching staff. My main goal was to get into their offices to learn from them. I knew that none of our scholarship players were owed anything by Coach O'Brien, and he probably didn't know any of them very well either. I figured building a rapport with the staff would help them see how much I wanted to be a part of the team and how much I wanted to improve.

I spent hours in Dave Spiller's office. He was a player's coach and showed a desire to build relationships with us. He frequently made "mix tapes" of players he thought we played like and should emulate our play after. The tape he made for me had highlight after highlight of Keith Van Horn from the University of Utah. I appreciated this comparison, as he was one of the best players in college basketball at the time. He and the other assistants took to calling me a "poor man's Keith Van Horn," which was fine by me. I was glad to get noticed and have someone care about me improving as a player.

SUMMER GROWTH

I wasn't headed to Walt Disney World that summer. As much as I would have liked to go back to Orlando, the inspiring confidence builder that it was, I couldn't. I needed to be in Columbus. I had to continue to learn from our coaches, play against talented players, and generally soak up all things basketball-related. I took an internship position with a well-known rental car company. I had heard how competitive their positions were and that they hired former athletes because of their resiliency and competitiveness. This sounded like a perfect match for me as I began the summer.

Wrong.

It wasn't a perfect match. In fact, it wasn't even close to a perfect match. I dreaded going to work there. It was a stellar company, but it was not the "Happiest Place on Earth." After all of the previous summer's excitement helping ecstatic Disney vacationers, working daily with people who had to get a rental vehicle because their car broke down or they had gotten into an accident was a real downer.

The position had me doing everything their entry level employees did, but that didn't make the job exhilarating. I wore a suit (the one Coach Ayers had made me buy), but was still vacuuming out rental cars for customers in the ninety-five-degree heat. While my perspiration increased, people complained about not getting the rate they wanted or the vehicle they were promised. A good day consisted of driving to pick up cars from another location or picking up someone from the airport. The tradeoff was fighting traffic for a few minutes of air conditioning. Any way you slice it, those were long days of monotonous work.

Speaking of long days, I was working full-time and still trying to put the effort in to become a better basketball player. Here is how my schedule looked:

6 a.m.–8 a.m.: Lift weights
8 a.m.–9 a.m.: Eat, shower, drive to work
9 a.m.–6:30 p.m.: Internship with the rental car company
6:30 p.m.–7:30 p.m.: Drive home, eat, change
for basketball
7:30 p.m.–9:30 p.m.: Conditioning and basketball workout

Fatigued is a mildly descriptive word for how I felt each night. The two-hour lifting sessions and mounting work stress were pretty deflating by the end of the day. Still, I urgently wanted to improve, so I frequently headed to the Jessie Owens Recreation Hall on South Campus as the evening set in. The recreation center was built like an old airplane hangar, and it hadn't been updated in decades. Originally the facility had four indoor basketball courts that had a surface like a tennis court and could be converted. At some point, they dumped weight lifting equipment and treadmills on two of the courts. It was a makeshift, ancient facility with no air conditioning—or air flow for that matter. On the bright side, it was close to my apartment, wind resistant, and usually sparsely populated. I could walk to it easily and get some shots up or add in some conditioning.

My standard plan was to come in and look to see if there was a basketball game with even remotely decent talent. If so, I would jump in to get some game action. I wasn't a fan of running just to run, so even a low-level game made the workout more interesting. When there was no game or the court had too many teams waiting, I ran on a treadmill to earn my chance to shoot. I tried to make a habit of attacking the thing I liked least on my "to do" list first. Once that was finished, everything else seemed easier.

After my run, I would head over to an open court to shoot, which is still one of my favorite things to do in the world. Often, the activity wasn't even about shooting but the chance to think about whatever I wanted. Shooting hoops was my ultimate stress release, and I enjoyed the chance to think through my day and work through any obstacles that needed to be addressed.

Shooting rarely got old. I shot inside, outside, back to the basket, you name it. I'd pick a certain move and try it over and over again. The repetition made the move muscle memory after hundreds and eventually thousands of attempts. I enjoyed the rhythm. This was something I had control over, and I knew if I put in the work I would get better. I started really seeing improvement after I wasn't afraid to fail. I'd push myself to go faster until I lost the ball, which helped me increase the speed at which I played.

I looked forward to that time every day. I shot or played until about 9:30 p.m., then headed home to start it all over again. When weekends came, I rarely went out or did much because I was so drained from the work week. Rest was crucial to staying motivated, and the weekend held my only free minutes to recharge. Still, the repetitive nature began to wear on me after weeks and weeks.

STAYING HUNGRY

A new source of motivation came one night after all the lifting, car cleaning, driving, running, and finally shooting was almost finished. I was keeping to myself on one of the back courts at the Jessie Owens South Facility when a guy I'd never met walked up to me. Initially I thought he might ask if I would play the next game with him. He was pretty tall and looked the part of a player, so I was about to take him up on it, except that wasn't at all what he asked me.

He said, "Aren't you on the team?"

I followed with a simple "Yeah."

This was starting out like a conversation I'd had many times before. Other students would ask what it was like playing on the team or mention they had a link to another Buckeye player. I was waiting for him to unveil his connection or coincidence, but I was again totally wrong about his intentions. He had a different agenda, and he wanted me to be crystal clear on it. He said simply and directly, "I'm going to take your spot."

Then he walked away. I was taken aback by his bold statement. That wasn't the comment I expected at all—not even close. I did a double take thinking, *Was that really what he said?*

I continued to shoot a little longer while processing his statement. Finally, I formulated an opinion on what had transpired. I said to myself, *Thank you. Thank you for feeding me some extra motivation to push through the rest of the summer and also giving me an extra goal to shoot for: outworking that guy.* Whether he actually had a chance to beat me out or not was insignificant. Actually, I never saw him again. Even today, I couldn't identify him if you placed him in a line up. His words, however, were exactly what I needed. The all too real vision that others out there were hungry to be where I was made me a more desperate player. This was the perfect carrot to keep me focused until tryouts.

BLIND AMBITION

Getting an extra push while working out on my own was one thing, but I also needed to get quality game experience to take the next step. So, for the first time, I got an opportunity to play in the Worthington Summer League. This was one of the top summer leagues in the region, based on the talent that played each year. Players like Nick Van Exel, who played for six different NBA teams over a thirteen-year career played to stay in shape and prepare for the next season. On top of the NBA talent, add in any college basketball player from the central Ohio area who was home for the summer. This included players like James Posey from Xavier, who eventually played for more than a decade in the NBA. Finally, throw in every current and former Buckeye who was still lacing up their sneakers, and you had a heck of a summer league. The talent was so rich that the general public would often show up in large numbers to watch. I couldn't ask for better summer competition.

I played on a team that did a good job of encouraging team basketball. We had guys from Ohio University, Miami of Ohio, Kent State University, and Don Jantonio from our team. We moved the ball extremely well for a summer league team, and it was a great experience. One game early in the summer, I had thirty points. Afterward I had guys coming up asking me if I wanted to transfer to play somewhere else. They said they could get me scholarships to other schools. I said no thank you and walked away. I had more to do as a Buckeye, and I was sold on staying there to achieve it.

The most memorable game of the summer was against a team stacked with talent including a fairly high-profile player named Samaki Walker. Walker was a 6'9" Columbus native who was home from Louisville. He was eventually the ninth pick in the NBA draft and played for ten years in the league, including a stint with the Los Angeles Lakers when they won back-to-back-to-back NBA titles. Ironically, I had asked him for his autograph when he and I were both in high school after his Whitehall team lost in the state championship game to none other than Girard. Now I wasn't asking for autographs, I was guarding him! For him, I'm sure this game was nothing special, but for me it was a mark of my growth as a player.

Early in the game I went for an offensive rebound, and an opposing player reached back to grab the ball and poked me in the eye. He had scratched my cornea, but I wouldn't find that out until the next day. At that moment, my vision was blurry. In retrospect, I think it distracted me from the moment just enough to help me not worry about my match up against a future pro. I am not sure if I had scored prior to the injury, but following it I had thirteen points. I even hit a three in the second half despite the blurriness. I was in the flow and feeling good about my game. I just couldn't see what was happening very well.

Afterward, I had to have Don's dad, who had come to watch him play, take my car home because I couldn't see well enough to drive. I found that if I looked around with my good eye, my scratched eye also moved. That was pretty painful, so I was relegated to closing both eyes for the time being. After a visit to the optometrist, I was to sit in the dark for two weeks with my eyes closed. Mostly, I listened to the radio and books on tape to escape boredom.

As much as I wanted and maybe needed a break, this was not how I wanted to get one. I felt like I was in a groove, really turning the corner with my play and wanted to get back on the court as soon as I could possibly get out there. I headed to the weight room throughout the experience and opened my eyes enough to move around and complete exercises. Looking back, I was fortunate I didn't cause the injury more trauma. In the moment, I couldn't help it. I was trying to do anything to keep myself building positive momentum.

CALORIE COUNT

One place I truly needed this momentum was at the dinner table. Even with impaired vision, I could still keep eating. And I had an urgent need to eat! My junior season, I had played at 195 pounds, which was robust compared to 175 pounds in my first season. I still lacked the girth to compete, especially because I found myself playing in the post more than anywhere else. Late in my junior campaign, after being pushed around like a shopping cart, I had finally had enough. It was time to do something.

During the spring quarter, I caught wind of the athletic department having a connection to a sports nutritionist. Athletes had the opportunity to meet them with questions or concerns. I always thought of a sports nutritionist as someone who helped players eat healthier and lose weight to get on the field. When someone says they are on a diet, that generally means they want to lose weight, right? I had never had a problem doing that. In fact, I lost weight without even trying. Putting on even an ounce was incredibly hard. For me, the lack of weight always held me back. Every single player on the court outweighed me by approximately thirty pounds. This had to change if I wanted to consistently compete.

I know many people would look at this and say that's not a problem. Just go and eat. But I was eating. I was eating a lot. My metabolism was so high, and we were working out so much, I felt like it took everything I could do to maintain my current weight. Any weight I had put on since I began college came during my year of depression after I was cut, when I was doing absolutely nothing. I couldn't sit around. I had to get better and get bigger.

After I'd made the connection that a sports nutritionist could potentially help me with my lack of weight, I made an appointment to meet with Beth Miller, a dietician and sports nutritionist working with our sports programs. The first task she had me accomplish was to write down everything I ate for a week and then take that list back to her so she could analyze my caloric intake. I followed her plan and then waited for a call back. A few days later she had me back in the office for a consultation.

Beth sat down with me to discuss my options. I think she could see my body language saying gaining weight was impossible. She immediately tried to grow my psychological energy. She said, "This is going to be exciting! Normally I meet with gymnasts or wrestlers who are trying hard to keep weight off or to lose several pounds in a healthy manner to improve performance or maintain their weight class. You have a more enjoyable problem. Since you are trying to gain weight, part of the solution is going to be that you get to eat whatever you want!"

She told me she had averaged out the calories I had eaten. She said I was eating approximately 4,000 calories each day to maintain my current weight. Keep in mind a standard healthy diet measures 2,500 calories. This should give an indication of how much I had to consume to just to keep being me. My metabolism was through the roof!

She went on to tell me that a pound is the equivalent of 3,500 calories. For me to gain one pound per week, I would need to eat about 4,500 calories per day. I needed an extra 500 calories over what I had been taking in. If I did this for seven days in a row, I would gain one pound that week.

While it was great to hear that I could eat whatever I wanted, I knew this would be a tremendous amount of work. I also knew that once fall conditioning started and preseason practice began, I would only be able to maintain weight. We would burn upwards of 5,000 calories per day, so at that stage I would need to follow a similar eating pattern to maintain the weight I had put on.

I looked at the amount of time before we started fall conditioning. I thought I had about sixteen weeks to focus all my extra time and energy on gaining weight. That meant I could put on about sixteen pounds if all went as planned. On the surface, it did sound enjoyable. We are talking about eating anything and everything I saw. Who wouldn't get excited about that kind of dietary plan?

It sounded great in theory, but I felt like I was already eating like crazy to keep up. Now I would have to step it up even more. The team had approximately four hours of workouts each day that included lifting, running, games, and skill work. I couldn't eat for about two hours leading up to a session, because I would toss it back up. I tried diligently to get eight to nine hours of sleep for muscle recovery. With either work or classes taking a sizable chunk of the rest of my time, I was basically looking at having to eat at any free moment.

Eating became a second job for me, and the tabulation took forever as well. I couldn't just hope I was getting 5,000 calories a day. I had to write down everything I ate, look up in a book the number of calories in each item and add it all up. Portion sizes made an accurate count tricky. For example, I would have to figure out if the bowl of cereal I ate was actually a "bowl" or two bowls or how many ounces it weighed. When I had a casserole, all bets were off. Who really knows what a casserole holds from a caloric perspective? Unless I made the casserole from scratch, which I didn't, I had no idea what the overall content of the meal was. The accounting work was frustrating enough if I actually knew what the calories were for each item I consumed.

If only they'd had apps back then!

I couldn't take a meal off or ever eat light or I wouldn't have enough calories to gain weight. Often, I would wait until the end of the night to add up the day's meals in an attempt to condense my tabulation time. Many days I was completely full at 10 p.m., but when I finally tallied my caloric intake, I had eaten only 4,000 calories. My choices were to not gain weight that day, or to cram down some more food. I couldn't afford to not gain weight. Letting even a day here or there go by without hitting my calorie count would destroy my chances of putting on weight. So, I searched for something else to eat that I hoped wouldn't make me vomit. Sometimes, I would sit up for a couple of hours until I had enough room to jam down more food.

I enjoyed some fun moments during the weight gaining process. One time I went to a casual restaurant to eat with a buddy, and when the server asked what I wanted to eat, I responded, "What item on your menu has the most calories?" She gave me a look like I had three heads. Then she answered, "No one has ever asked me that question before. I'll check." After a few minutes of discussion with other staff members, she came back and said their highest calorie item was, without question, the "garbage burger."

"Then that is what I'm having." My friend gave me a slightly odd look. I responded by explaining, "This is the best way to order food when trying to gain weight!" We both chuckled, and then I ate the garbage burger. I quickly found out why it had the most calories. I get full just thinking about that sandwich.

LESSON EARNED

As fall conditioning began, I weighed in at 210 pounds. I had successfully put on fifteen pounds in the offseason. I would give back about five of these pounds during all the running of the preseason, but that was still a huge gain for me.

I would still be a good bit lighter than the majority of my opponents, but this was much better than where I was previously. I could literally feel the difference on every play. I felt stronger, and I was able to absorb hits better. Most importantly, I had achieved a goal that I had worked hard to accomplish. Now I looked forward to benefiting from my new size and strength as my senior year began.

Overall, my weight was up, my play was improving, and my strength and agility were on the upswing as I started the fall. Our coaches took notice as well. I was finally able to begin the fall weights and conditioning program with the team. No more walk-on tryouts for me. I was thankful to be a full-time member of the program, and I planned to make the most of this opportunity. As we tested out for the fall and began our transition into preseason practice, I was able to pass all of our fall conditioning times, including our less-than-twelve-minute, two-mile run. I had increased my bench press max to 265 pounds. Now I was encouraging younger players as a leader during our workouts.

Most memorably, I tested out having the highest vertical leap on the team. Now I probably should clarify that I think most of the guys mailed in their effort because we were tested after a lifting session, conditioning, and open gym. When they called us over to French Field House after all that, the look of disgust on all players' faces showed. Our body language screamed that fatigue had already set in. Still, a chance to show how far I had come in such an important basketball measure had me locked in to the competition. In the end, a win was a win. I beat out Scoonie Penn by a half inch. In his defense, Scoonie was battling a deep thigh bruise. In mine, I was battling shin splints. Nevertheless, I was thrilled with the victory and all of my strength and conditioning gains. I felt I had shown that I could hang with all the scholarship players athletically, something that proved to be a drastic separation point in the past.

If I learned one thing from this entire process, it was that if I don't find my failure point, I won't continue to improve. We must begin to embrace a little bit of failure. It's amazing what can happen in life when failure is an opportunity instead of something to avoid. A whole new world of growth is available to anyone who makes this discovery.

I believe Coach O'Brien also saw the progress I had made because part way through the fall quarter, when I walked into his office, he awarded me a scholarship for the remainder of the academic year. This was yet another sign of achievement that I was granted. I was now a scholarship Big Ten athlete with lots of optimism going into my final season. I also had a great deal of confidence. I felt like I had earned the opportunity that awaited me.

CHAPTER 9
Senior Season

As my fifth year of school and my final season of eligibility began, I was bigger, stronger, and more skilled. I badly wanted to be a more visibly valuable member of the team. Making the team picture that season was one sign that I had progressed. The day we lined up to take the photo was gratifying. For the first time in my Ohio State career, I wasn't sitting on the side watching or still trying out. Yet, I hoped to make a bigger impact on the court. To this point, I had played in only six games in two seasons and had scored only one free throw, with minimal statistics in any categories to show for all my efforts. I hoped to make it into the rotation for good this season and factor into each game.

During our first exhibition game, I subbed in off the bench and played terribly. In a few minutes of action, I believe I had two turnovers and no highlights. I was devastated. I believed I had lost a spot in the rotation. This was probably the opinion of our coaches as well. Suddenly, Kwadjo, who was a good friend and back for his second season on the team, was getting minutes in front of me. I felt like I was getting passed over, so I started to get frustrated. I began worrying about who was playing in front of me. I wondered what each coach was thinking and why I wasn't getting another opportunity. Basically, I started worrying about a bunch of issues I couldn't control. This is a challenge everyone works through in life. At the moment, I was not dealing with it very well. I was actually missing my opportunity while worrying about it.

Not only did I worry about things I couldn't control, I worried about selfish things like, "Why am I not playing?" or "Why am I not starting?" I should have been asking, "What can I do to improve?" or "How can I help the team?" These are the kinds of questions that help anyone who is doing poorly get back on track and embrace the process. As it was, I didn't even ask for any answers. I never once went to my coaches to find out what else I could do to improve. Had I done this, I could have set better goals and direction in my time of frustration. Then I could have enjoyed the first few months of the season much more.

This displaced frustration caused me to miss out on some real enjoyment during my senior season. I played with loads of pent up anger instead of just doing the best I could on the next play. We started out a solid 7–3 and had one of the best freshmen in the country in Michael Redd. I should have been enjoying being a part of that good start. However, I was not mentally focused on playing my best basketball, and without that, no amount of physical effort or hustle was going to be enough. I needed a spark to refocus my mental energy.

To make matters worse, my focus and our season were both going to get worse before they got better. Over the Christmas holiday we flew to Hawaii to play in the Rainbow Classic. We were going to play the number-one-ranked University of Kansas team that was loaded with talent. We played the Jayhawks very close and were within a couple of possessions of them with about five minutes to go. Then,

Paul Pierce, a future Celtic great who is considered a lock to be inducted into the basketball hall of fame, decided to take over the game. The result was a thirteen-point loss in a contest that was much closer than the final score. What should have been a potential springboard for us to show we could play with the big boys turned into a nightmare when we lost to New Mexico State on day two. Finally, on the third straight day, we played in the dreaded seventh place game against Brigham Young University (BYU). That game would determine which team would salvage a win before heading home.

The 11:00 a.m. game had about three hundred people in attendance, and the crowd and public interest made it feel like a high school summer league game. Our performance was as quiet as the gym was. It was so quiet, in fact, I couldn't help but hear a guy heckling Coach O'Brien from about ten rows up. After the game, Coach O'Brien gave it back to the guy and appeared to have every intention of going after him before our assistants stopped him from heading in the stands.

I liked that Coach O'Brien was about to fight for us. We had dropped to 7–6 and were the only team in Hawaii not to get a win that week. In some ways, his actions showed he wasn't giving up and he wasn't going to just lie down and take the abuse without going down swinging. On the other hand, two days ago we had a decent record and played right along with one of the best teams in the country. Were the wheels really coming off the wagon? It appeared we were all getting desperate to right the ship!

Individually, I had hit a low as well. I had played in the New Mexico State game, a 27-point loss to a relatively average basketball team at best. I was in as bad a fog as I had ever been as a player. I was caught up thinking about why I wasn't put in the game earlier and why certain teammates were playing in front of me. I was frustrated that I wasn't getting "real minutes" instead of looking at every minute of game play as a real minute and a chance to help our team or make a memorable play. Something needed to change and soon, or I was not going to finish my career the way I wanted.

MENTAL EDGE

I was nowhere near the player or person I wanted to be mentally. No one wants to live angry. Enjoying basketball and being a part of all that comes with it was the focal point I had to find again. I was searching for something to change my mindset and get me going. I had worked so hard to change myself physically and athletically, I needed a mental spark to pull it all together.

The spark I needed did not come from a shot I made, an act of good will, or encouragement by a coach. In fact, my senior year turning point came from a statement from someone who might never have picked up a basketball. Up until now, in what sometimes felt like an afterthought, our team had scheduled a few meetings with sports psychologists Todd Kays and Chris Stankovich. Both were hired by OSU to work with athletic teams, and they came in to work with us as our season began to slide downhill. The team met for a couple of sessions here and there to address the mental aspect of the game. During one of our meetings, a comment was made that finally became my tipping point. Dr. Stankovich said, "If you would like to schedule individual appointments with us, it could really change your mental approach to the game. Think about it. You wouldn't go in the weight room once a month and have the expectation of getting physically stronger, would you? The same applies to the mental side of the game."

Well said.

His statement immediately got my attention. I had seen the benefits of a disciplined weight program. I had seen what a diet monitored daily could do for my overall physique. A consistent and well directed focus had to be what I was missing to improve my mental performance. That was it. I was committed. I scheduled an individual meeting in an effort to change my mental momentum.

At my first appointment, we discussed my frustrations and how so many of my worries were things beyond my control. We talked about how spending time on those thoughts took away the opportunity to spend time on things I could control. We also talked about what it was going to take to improve my performance. Visualization was a huge part of that correction. Prior to meeting with Chris and Todd, I thought listening to relaxing music and envisioning yourself performing well seemed kind of silly. After we met, my thoughts shifted 180 degrees.

I learned that visualization is truly the starting point of success. Players who say their "shot is off today" or they "can't stop that guy" are already beaten. To combat these thoughts, I started to take to heart a famous Henry Ford quote: "Whether you think you can or you can't, you're probably right."

In order to live by this quote during these mental training sessions, it was crucial to visualize myself doing well and succeeding in the task at hand. Visualizing only positive events would breed the confidence necessary to succeed. There is a reason why "perfect practice makes perfect" is a popular statement. However, success needs to happen in your mental preparation before it can be carried out physically. Not only are you getting perfect repetitions during mental preparation, but you are doing so without any wear and tear on your body.

I have no idea why more coaches don't encourage this kind of practice routinely with their players. Maybe it is because coaches can't see into players' heads to make sure they are running the play correctly. I view it this way: during my senior season, we played at Michigan, Iowa, and Penn State all in a five day stretch. There was often minimal practice time and even less time for physical recovery. So, there was a huge benefit to getting those mental repetitions. Offensively, our team could imagine running a completely new play designed to take advantage of the weaknesses we'd noticed since the last time we played that opponent. Defensively, the more our team could mentally replicate guarding an opposing team's offense and the specific plays they ran, the better chance we'd have to stop them. We could make one or two days feel more like a week of preparation.

Tremendous comfort came from this visualization. Generally, players watch plenty of films and highlights designed to remind them what they are like when they make really good plays, but rarely in my career did we spend time visualizing what the next day's game would look like or spend time envisioning ourselves in that setting. Almost everybody subscribes to the notion of a home court advantage. Why is that? The home team has support from the energy of their fans. They didn't have the travel of the visiting team and they are familiar with the rims, floor, and specifically the shooting background. I believe being comfortable with what a person is looking at when shooting and the individual's depth perception based on the bleachers behind the rim has a profound impact on shooting percentages.

Alex Suchman wrote a blog in 2014 that suggested NBA teams were shooting .75 percent better from the free throw line at home that year. Think about that for a second. A free throw is called that for a reason. It's free!

The distance is always the same, and there is no defense. So what changes? The main differences would be crowd noise, shooting background, and general comfort. If players have the opportunity to visualize that setting prior to actually playing, doesn't that improve their chances of success?

As I became more proficient at visualization, I also became a more relaxed player. I started to overcome the discomfort of unfamiliar gyms and high-profile players. Mental preparation helped me gain the repetition I wasn't getting during games.

One of the key ingredients in this growth was watching film with our coaches. No one was better at this than our associate head coach, Rick Boyages. Coach Boyages was one of the nicest, most caring, and most knowledgeable coaches I have ever worked with in my basketball career. He also pretty much lived in the film room. I loved film as well, so I made a habit of getting in to watch with him whenever I could. He never said, "Sorry, Eric, but you can't sit in on this one. It is a coaches' only session." Whether he was watching us or a future opponent, he talked me through what he was seeing whenever we were together. I believe I learned as much from him in a year of watching tape as I probably did from any other coach. To aid my success with visualization, watching film gave me the plays, the players, and the places I needed to see to get extra mental practice. I would use these visuals to take my game to the next level for the second half of my senior year.

Hanging out with Coach Boyages was an incredible basketball education. Frequently he stopped the film and asked questions like, "What's wrong with this possession?" or "What caused that turnover?" Good players anticipate what is going to happen next. Great players frequently see about three steps ahead. Learning from watching film increased my understanding of the game's little nuances. I began to value a pass fake or the angle of a screen as much as any basketball skill.

I also gained a much better understanding of the strategies of our opponents. It wasn't like I hadn't watched film before, but I never felt welcomed to digest all of it. I had never before been given the opportunity to ask questions as the tape rolled. I had loved basketball before, but I was finding a new level of understanding. I began to envision myself coaching the game after I graduated. For now, I had unfinished business as a player.

FIGHT ON

After the frustration of going 0–3 in Hawaii, we were still a game over .500 and heading back to Columbus to play Wisconsin at home to open the Big Ten season. In a hard-fought, close contest, we came up on the short end, 64–59. I still wasn't playing, but my mind was getting closer to being in the right place. I was enjoying what I knew was my last go-around in the Big Ten. Make no mistake, I hadn't given up. I still wanted to play and win, but I wasn't going to worry about things I couldn't control. No longer would I worry about what a coach was thinking or why someone was playing in front of me. I was going to focus on doing the best I could on the next play, whether it was in a game or practice. I was going to soak up the enjoyment of being a part of a team and improving my relationships with my teammates. As I did, I not only enjoyed the game more, but the relationships I built helped me become a better player. No teammate had more to do with this development than Scoonie Penn.

Scoonie was sitting out the 1997–1998 season because of transfer rules, but he still did everything with us. I could immediately tell after meeting him that taking the year off was the last thing on his mind. He wanted to get better. Scoonie would grab anyone who wanted to work hard and work with them. He and I played one-on-one daily. We might have seemed like an odd match up with me being about 6'7" and him being about 5'11". People probably thought I would back him down and shoot over him in the post or he would dribble around me and get to the rim all day. Both might have been true in an open game, but we played with a two-dribble limit, making both of those options impossible. The two-dribble rule was Scoonie's rule, and he imposed it because he said players get only about two dribbles in half-court offense before the defense collapses on the dribbler and takes it.

This made sense as he explained it, so I was all in for playing that way. We also moved to different spots on the floor for our games. Sometimes we would play from the wing or the corner. We wanted to practice from all the spots where we might get a one-on-one opportunity in a game and not just from the top of the key. This kept the game fresh and improved my comfort all over the floor. The realistic nature of the drill improved my ability to perform.

I never knew how much a player could do with two dribbles until we started those games, nor did I realize how much ground I could cover when putting the ball on the floor only twice. We played first to three points by ones, so neither one of us was really ever out of a game. This made us play hard throughout. One of the best parts of these one-on-one games was how competitive Scoonie was when he played. His energy level was higher than anyone I had ever been around, and it forced me to raise my level or be embarrassed that I didn't.

Scoonie and I (frequently joined by Kwadjo) battled in shooting drills after our regular practice was over. We shot from different spots, had free throw contests, and even played an occasional game of Dribble King in the center circle. Scoonie made working at the game fun while showing the intensity needed in every practice and every drill to get better.

My confidence grew exponentially, not only because I was building skills, but because Scoonie cared enough to push me. Feeling valued by a teammate with his level of prominence meant the world to me. My belief in my abilities was at an all-time high. It was time to carry that belief over to practices and games.

While the three of us constantly battled after practice, during practice we were teammates. Kwadjo, Scoonie, Byron Wilson, and I were constantly together on the scout team. Our team of five would be rounded out with one more player that switched daily, depending on who coach O'Brien decided to rotate in with the first unit. Scoonie galvanized our group into one that never wanted to lose, no matter what the drill was. Day after day, our scout team kept winning. Scoonie's confidence fed us all belief. Aside from him, we were all afterthoughts out to prove we were every bit as good as the highly recruited scholarship players. We formed the type of special bond that helps teams become successful. Scoonie was the architect behind our bond. If Buckeye fans ever wonder what made him such a great and memorable player in Ohio State lore, the answer is pretty simple. Good players make themselves better. Great players make others better. Scoonie made every player on the floor with him far better than they ever thought they could be.

RENEWED CONFIDENCE

My belief as a player had risen to an all-time high. With a new mental focus, I was looking to make an impact every day. During one late season practice, we were in the middle of a one-on-one post drill where coaches entered the ball when a player established good position. It was a great drill to work on offensive and defensive positioning in the post. Coach O'Brien, who occasionally worked with the big guys, was throwing the ball in to the offensive player. The intensity of the drill usually ramped up when the head coaches' eyes were on us.

The ball was swung around to Coach O'Brien, who then passed it into me while John Lumpkin was on defense. I turned middle, and realized I was a lot closer to the rim than I expected. John had solid defensive position, but at that moment I felt really strong, so I went up to score with authority. I exploded upward and dunked the ball straight through him. John was really surprised. I am not sure he thought I was even capable of making such a play (which might have helped me convert it). I'm not sure I thought I was capable of it either. Nonetheless, that basket caused a noticeable reaction from the players looking on. John gave Coach O'Brien a bewildered look. Coach responded by saying, "What do you want me to do about it? Step up your game!"

Later on that week, we were practicing a two-on-one drive and dish drill. The guard dribbled in as if he had beat his man near the foul line. He decided whether to score or pass based on what the lone defender did. I was in the short corner and readied myself to turn and score if the ball was passed to me. Twice in a row, Scoonie dribbled in and dropped the ball off to me. Twice in a row I went over Byron Wilson, the lone defender and hammered down dunks. The first time drew a reaction from the team. The second time, it completely stopped practice. So emphatic were both dunks that Coach O'Brien had to stop everything and say something to lift Byron's spirits. He bellowed, "Let them laugh now Byron, but you are the toughest guy in this gym, and I know there isn't a player in here who would want to meet you in a back alley."

I was glad Coach had said that to him. Byron was one of my favorite teammates, and I didn't want to see him get torn up by the rest of the crew, especially when he was giving a full effort. I had my moment and didn't need any praise. The team's reaction showed me they were impressed with my play. It was a brief moment in practice, but it proved how far I had come as a player. Four years earlier, Antonio Watson had me wondering if I could ever adjust to this level of play. Now I was the one making the plays happen.

I was firing on all cylinders mentally on and off the court. I had earned a 4.0 GPA during the fall quarter while taking senior level business classes. I was finishing a triple major in marketing, operations management, and transportation and logistics. My grades were a far cry from the 2.75 GPA I salvaged in the first quarter I played. I was finished scrambling to get things done, and I was prepared. Coach O'Brien made a point to tell me how proud he was of my efforts to represent our team so well in the classroom. This was a huge confidence boost for me proving my life changes extended beyond basketball.

The Big Ten season started off rocky and we hoped to change our fortunes during a mid-January home game against Michigan. They were loaded with talent, including Robert "Tractor" Traylor, a 6'9", 290-pound anomaly of size and athletic ability who would play for years in the NBA because of those attributes. To put things in perspective, my very own mother claimed she had "scouted" Michigan for me on television and said Traylor was "too big for me to play against."

Thanks, Mom.

There I was trying like crazy to do anything to get on the court, and my own mother was trying to bench me!

The game was lopsided. I don't remember feeling our team was within shouting distance at any point in the second half. My number was finally called to go in to the game during what is often called "garbage time." That was no longer my outlook on this portion of the game. If I had even five seconds of playing time, I was going to make the most of it. I had new confidence and new focus. I was energized to take advantage of any opportunity.

Down twenty-one points on the scoreboard, with under ten seconds to go, we were walking the ball up the floor, and I called for it, seeing that the time was melting away. My defender was several feet away since I was a good distance beyond the three-point arc. I caught the pass in rhythm and let it fly. The ball went through the hoop barely touching the bottom of the net as the buzzer sounded. The loudest cheer of the afternoon went up from those who still remained in attendance. The hard-core fans who had stayed until the last few moments of the game had been waiting all day for something to get excited about, and finally they had it. After quickly shaking hands I sprinted into the locker room so fast that I was the only one there. I was so energized, I wished there was more game to be played. Overall, I was excited that I had maximized my opportunity to make something good happen no matter how small a window I was given.

For a long time after that game people came up to me on the street and said they remembered my deep three against Michigan. Of course the details got slightly exaggerated, even in other people's memories. They'd say, "Nice half-court shot verses the Wolverines!" I always smiled and said thanks even though their memory wasn't close to accurate. I couldn't believe so many people watched and appreciated my play. It wasn't like my effort won the game. It cut our loss from a twenty-one-point drubbing to a slightly less obscene eighteen-point defeat. Still, I think the comments reflected how much Buckeye fans appreciated any progress against the "team up North" and how loyal they were as they watched the entire dreadful performance. My first basket from the field as a Buckeye was a life lesson in action. I was beginning to take advantage of every opportunity I earned.

Our Big Ten season continued and so did our struggles. We were playing a late January road game against Minnesota and the losses began to wear on us. At one point, Coach O'Brien was beside himself with anger during a time out because we had allowed Sam Jacobson to play deep into a lopsided game without anyone toughening up against him as he continued to pile up big numbers. With about three minutes to go, Coach O'Brien hollered down the bench to have me enter the game. With my newfound mental approach, I looked at these minutes as an opportunity. No longer was I letting the scoreboard dictate my body language and play. I entered into the game looking to make something happen. In those fleeting moments, I grabbed three rebounds, one of which I purposefully tapped to Kwadjo all in one motion for an easy layup. In the locker room after the game, Coach O'Brien yelled to Ken Johnson, "Ken, you played thirty plus minutes tonight and had one rebound. Eric played three minutes and tripled that! Maybe we should rethink who is playing on this team!"

A few months earlier, I would have read too far into his statement. With a new mental approach, I was not going to get too high or too low about what a coach was thinking.

That consistently burned me in the past. It was nice to get a little carrot of praise, but with my new mental focus, I looked for the next opportunity to show I could play.

It's a good thing I didn't get too worked up about Coach O'Brien's praise, because it didn't translate into much change. Ken was a 6'11" freshman with a thirty-one-inch plus vertical leap who could run like a deer. It would have been inexcusable for them to move away from his development. Coach was trying to light a fire under Ken to get him playing harder. Ken was a raw talent and the future of our team. He had to play, especially if we couldn't find another way to win games now. Ken could be a game changer—and would be—by the time he ended his playing career. He finished his time at Ohio State as the all-time leading shot blocker in Big Ten history thanks to his efforts, and our coaching staff who continually pushed him. I give Coach O'Brien and his staff tremendous credit for molding Ken into an impressive player by the time he finished his Buckeye playing days.

MAKING AN IMPACT

My focus on maximizing every opportunity was gaining notice from our coaching staff. A week or so later during practice, we were scrimmaging five-on-five, and Jason Singleton was guarding me. A shot went up from the corner, and I went to rebound it and to look for a put back. On this particular play, Jason got caught up in defensive rotations and wasn't able to get back to me to box out. I ran in untouched from the corner as the shot came from the opposite wing. I leaped up and caught the ball in the air as it bounced off the back of the rim and caromed toward the free throw line. As I caught the ball, it was slightly behind my body. I was perpendicular to the basket, but I managed to reach out with my left hand and dunk the ball behind my head. Never before or since have I had a one-handed tip dunk that was even close to resembling that one. The play was an aberration, a true combination of timing, good fortune, and definitely luck.

It was an unparalleled rush.

Coach O'Brien couldn't help but take notice. Immediately, he had me flip my reversible jersey over to the color the first team was wearing. This was an enormous individual moment because I rarely, if ever, took reps on the first team. During the very next play, I was again crashing the boards on the right side of the court. I caught a missed shot from the left wing and I tip-dunked that rebound as well. This dunk wasn't nearly as impressive, but it was still a clear statement that I was ready for this moment. That play immediately made me feel like I belonged with the first group. With only a few games remaining, I had to show my abilities now or never.

The games continued, and the losses mounted. What made things worse was we still hadn't won a Big Ten game. I played a minute here or there at the end of a few blow outs but no long stretches. I kept my positive mindset and looked for opportunities wherever I could find them. I finally broke through in a twenty-six-point loss at the hands of Michigan State. We were out of the game entirely after the first five minutes of the second half, and Coach O'Brien gave me a much earlier call than usual. I am not sure if he was fed up with the usual rotation and looking for a spark or resting some high minute players. Who knows, maybe it was all of the above. Regardless, I was ready to play. I notched a career high of twelve minutes. While I had no real stats during that stretch, I played solid and kept our coaches interested in my ability to contribute. When I was watching the film with Coach Boyages the next day, he commented that I was the most fundamentally sound player on the court for either team during the stretch that I was in the game. He made me feel like my minutes were valuable even if I didn't fill up the stat sheet. His statement also confirmed that I was someone they could trust to be on the floor during any stretch of the game.

Our team kept losing, but I kept growing my conviction. I felt like I had my mind in the right place. During tough times, most people look at themselves as either the victim or the hero of their story. I was done being the victim. I wanted to go the hero route. I also generally believe people are either inflators or deflators by nature. When we see someone for even a few seconds, they can often elevate our day or bring it down solely by this brief interaction. I planned to be someone who lifted up people around me. I didn't care how many games in a row we lost. I was going to keep fighting.

We had seventeen consecutive defeats that included a heartbreaking loss at home in overtime against Indiana by a lone basket, 74–72. We had the ball with only a few seconds left and a chance to win, but we threw a pass away that was taken the distance for an uncontested, game winning dunk. Next, we headed to Madison to play the Badgers for our last road game of the year. Our team was desperate for a victory, as we were still searching for our first Big Ten and calendar year win. The Badgers had just opened their new facility, the Kohl Center, in the middle of the year. It was exciting to play in a brand-new arena where only a handful of games had been played.

By then, I had found a groove with my mental training. I spent time each evening visualizing myself in the next basketball setting or the next classroom and having success overall in that next moment. I gave myself the opportunity to achieve perfect practice and gain comfort in each new and unfamiliar environment. This upcoming game with

Wisconsin was the perfect opportunity to show how much progress I had made. We went into the Kohl Center the morning of the game for our standard pregame shootaround. I might have seen the arena on television once before and a little on tape in preparation for the game, but I really had very little familiarity with the court. By the time the game started, that would change significantly.

I really soaked in the background while we shot around and went through our set plays for the game. Once I had these visions in my head, the real preparation began. We went back to our hotel rooms for the afternoon prior to going to a short film session with our coaches. Then we would head off to pre-game meal. During our down time, I relaxed and visualized the game happening. I saw myself wearing our road uniforms against Badger players in the Kohl Center filled with fans. I saw myself playing well in that environment, running plays to perfection and doing the little things necessary to help our team have success. When we started to warm up for the game, it was as if I had already played it. I felt like the Kohl Center was my home gym, and I played there all the time. In fact, since Wisconsin had played there for only a little over a month, I felt like there was a pretty good chance I was as comfortable in their gym as they were. This was the moment when I became 100 percent sold on mental training. The calm I felt in such a new environment was unparalleled by any previous experience.

My comfort paid off early in the game, because I went in during the first half and had an immediate impact. Within the first few possessions, I scored a bucket on a scramble play near the basket. I also grabbed a rebound and made an immediate drop pass to a cutting teammate for a layup. Then I snagged another rebound and logged another assist. I was contributing, and we were winning.

I had played well enough that I got another rotation in the second half. In all, I played ten minutes racking up two points, two rebounds, two assists, and a steal. Neshaun Coleman, Michael Redd, and Jon Sanderson hit all their free throw attempts down the stretch, and we went home with a 61–56 win.

We were so excited about finally getting our first win in eighteen tries that one of our guys tossed a chair across the locker room and took a chunk out of their new drywall way up near the ceiling. Fortunately for that player, our coaching staff hadn't entered the locker room yet. A minute or so later, Coach O'Brien and the rest of the staff entered the locker room, and we shared a long overdue moment of joy together. We finally had a Big Ten win. Now it was time to head home for senior night and even more importantly, the last game in the history of St. John Arena.

MAKING HISTORY

St. John Arena opened in November of 1956 as a state-of-the-art basketball facility. Even in 1998, days from seeing its last basketball game, most division one teams would have traded to use it for their own arena in a heartbeat. There is something very special about any facility that is built specifically for your sport to be played and no other. It makes that place endearing to those who play there. A gym like St. John Arena feels like home. To this day, I frequently hear Buckeye fans say they wish we still played there.

As impressive as it was structurally, the list of talent that had called the arena home is even greater than the stature of the venue itself. It began with Ohio State being crowned National Champions in 1960 with names like Jerry Lucas, John Havlicek, Larry Siegfried, Mel Nowell, Joe Roberts, and Bobby Knight aiding the charge. It moved forward with players like Gary Bradds, Bill Hoskett, Clark Kellogg, Jimmy Jackson and, while I was playing, Michael Redd. It had witnessed amazing visiting opponents such as Lew Alcindor (before he was Kareem Abdul-Jabbar), Quinn Buckner, Isaiah Thomas, and Glenn Robinson. Knowing all this, it was easy for me to get excited about playing there, even for practice. Now we were talking about taking the floor there for one last historic game in the facility. The event had been sold out since the day tickets went on sale. The athletic department had printed up special last game ticket stubs and programs. Regardless of the rocky season we had up until then, this was going to be a memorable night. For me, it was about to get even more memorable.

After the Wisconsin game, Coach O'Brien came up to me the next day in practice and said, "You are starting against Penn State." I looked around me to see whom he was talking to. When I realized I was the only one there, I said "okay" and kept shooting in the drill we were practicing. I was excited, but I also had a question. I had seen over the years how teams tend to start seniors on senior night out of respect to those players and their commitment to the program. I can see the reasoning behind that, but I wanted to play and win the game. I didn't need a token start if that wasn't part of the plan for success. Heck, I didn't start senior night in high school, and we had five seniors! I was okay with being the only senior who didn't start then, and I still felt the same way. If my starting was part of our plan for success, then I was all for it. If not, put me in where it would help us succeed. I had to say something about it to our coaches. I began to think about how to bring this up to our staff so I didn't appear ungrateful.

The day before the game, prior to practice, I went into the facility and walked past Coach Boyages, who was watching film on Penn State. He was in the meeting room inside the locker room and had the door open. I sat down and watched with him as I normally did if I got there early enough. I hated to break our conversation on X's and O's, so I didn't say anything at first. Finally, when I was about to leave, I spoke up. The conversation went something like this.

Me: "Hey, coach. I wanted to ask you something."

Coach: "What's up, E?"

Me: "Well, it's about me starting against Penn State. I am very grateful for the opportunity and I want to play as much as I can to help the team, but that is just it. I don't want to start if it's not what is best to help our team win the game."

Coach: "Just so you know, we almost started you last game against Wisconsin. That's how much we think you can help our team right now."

Me: "Okay. Thanks, Coach. I'll do my best."

And that was it. I was starting. I believed him even if he said it only to get me on board with their plan of attack. I mean, why shouldn't I have believed him? He had always been honest with me. So, with new confidence that this was the best plan for us to win, I began to prepare for the big moment.

I felt like I was still doing well with my mental training, but it was pretty hard not to be nervous about the thought that I would start such an important game in Ohio State history. This was to be the final game in this historic place, and I not only had the honor of starting it, but I was the person jumping center for the opening tip. I really had trouble wrapping my brain around this fact. My first start ever in my entire basketball career would be the last start for this celebrated venue. This was going to take some serious mental preparation.

FINISH STARTING

The morning of the last game felt like daybreak on Christmas for any five-year-old who sends a wish list to Santa, times a thousand or so. I was more than excited, so much so that I had to take my mind completely away from the idea of playing the game. I went to the Tuttle Crossing Shopping Mall and walked around with some friends. I ran into former teammates, Don Jantonio and Rick Yudt. Both had graduated a year earlier and had come back into town to attend the game that night, along with almost every player who had ever donned the scarlet and gray. We stopped and talked for a few minutes about how important the game was to all the alumni who had played at Ohio State. Everyone wanted the building to be closed down the right way, with honor for all those who had played there. They wished me luck and moved on with their shopping.

So much for getting my mind off of the game.

Later on that afternoon, I was in the training room getting my ankles taped up to play. As Bords taped me up, we talked about all that he had seen in his thirty-one seasons at St. John Arena. He was yet another person I would be honoring while playing this game. As motivating as this thought was, it added to the drain I felt. I already felt a little fatigued, not so much from the mall walking but from the anxiety about the entirety of the situation. This was a concern, considering there were still a couple of hours until the game was supposed to start! I didn't even want to move. I needed all the energy I had left to get ready for the game, nervous energy or not.

Next up were the senior night festivities. I thought of how I wished my father were there, even though he never really connected with my desire for the game. I wished he could see the culmination of my hard work and passion. I wished we had taken the time to grow together. My mother walked out to the center of the court with me. All of the memories of her driving me to practices while I was growing up and supporting my interests came rushing back. She never once cared whether I played or not, or if she did, she never showed it. She came to support me because she knew I loved basketball. I thought of all the late nights she spent over the years making the three-hour trek back to Youngstown after watching us play. She always stayed after games to eat and visit, never once claiming she had to get back. I appreciated all of her sacrifice. It was truly a heartfelt moment.

I tried diligently to stay focused on the game. Coach O'Brien shook our hands and took pictures with each of us. Energy was buzzing around the sold-out arena, but it was also leaving my overly stimulated body at an alarmingly fast rate. This game couldn't start soon enough. I was already running on fumes.

Finally, we lined up for the opening tip. Because I was jumping center and playing the five spot, I had to guard Penn State's Calvin Booth, a Columbus native who hailed from Groveport Madison High School. He was a 6'11" senior who finished his career as the all-time leading shot blocker in the Big Ten. Cal was later drafted thirty-fifth overall by the Washington Wizards in the spring and went on to play in the NBA for ten years. The bad news was he had about four inches on me, and he was a very long player with uncanny timing. The good news was I played against him all the time in the summer. Our Worthington Summer League teams practiced against each other, so I was familiar with him as a player. That was the one thing that gave me comfort as the ball was tossed up to start a game at St. John Arena for the last time.

There wasn't an empty seat in the house. Camera flashes went off everywhere during the opening tip, and the contest had begun. Cal won the tip easily, and Penn State went on offense. I could tell they had talked about the size advantage Cal had over me, because they made a strong effort to get the ball to him early. To our team's credit, we also knew he had plenty of inches on me, so we were focused on trying to stop him. We held him pretty well in check during the early onset of the contest.

After several minutes, the horn sounded and Ken Johnson came over from the scorer's table to sub in for me. I took a seat on the bench to a nice round of applause. Had it not been for the last month of action, I would have assumed that my day was over. But with my change in mental focus, things were different. I had worked my way into the lineup and proved that when I was on the court, good things happened. Even the other guys on the team knew I was in the mix, because they willingly gave me a spot on the bench much closer to the scorer's table. I would sit up near the coaching staff when I was out of the game so I could be more connected to their game instruction. I felt great when everyone treated me like I belonged there.

A few minutes prior to half time, Coach O'Brien hollered my name. I jumped back up and subbed in. Almost immediately, we had an offensive possession where the ball was dished off to me very close to the basket. I went up to try and finish, but Calvin Booth sent my shot about three rows deep. (Since then, I often joke about how I was able to help him get the Big Ten blocks record.) We then inbounded the ball to Michael Redd, who pulled off one of his classic herky-jerky style moves that no one could ever figure out how to defend. After he left his defender standing flat footed, he began to slither through others and attacked the rim. He missed a short runner in the lane. I was able to corral the rebound and put it back in for my first two points of the game. As nervous and fatigued as I was, that was the energy shot I needed to get me going.

Soon after that, I was playing help side defense and a cutter came down the middle of the lane. He ran right through me in an attempt to knife toward the basket. After a few moments of discussion and lots of lobbying on Coach O'Brien's part, they called the Penn State player for a push, which sent me to the free throw line at the other end of the court. I made both ends of a one and one. Soon after that, I got fouled again and went back to the free throw line. This time I made one out of two attempts. The halftime buzzer sounded shortly afterward, and I went to the locker room with five points to my name and a defensive charge to boot as we went into the break with an early lead.

I was wound up. As we strategized in the locker room for the second half, the crowd worked itself into a frenzy as all the past letter winners in attendance took the court. Meanwhile Gene Millard, the player who made the first shot in arena history back in the 1950s, made a ceremonial last shot on his first attempt. Everyone was feeling good and ready for another exciting half of basketball. We had put a good half together but would need another quality half to hold on to our lead.

We went back out for the second half. Thanks in part to my first-half effort, I earned a handful of minutes and made the most of them. During a big run, I set a huge screen on a flair, allowing Neshaun Coleman to get wide open and nail a three. Then I collected another basket. Finally, while everything was going our way, Michael Redd drove in on the left side and dropped me a bounce pass. Calvin Booth had come over to help on Mike, which had given him just enough room to slip me the pass. I knew that I couldn't go up to shoot on the same side because Cal would block it into next week. I decided to swoop under the basket and shoot the ball on the other side of the rim. It felt like I hung in the air forever, but the rim shielded me, and the ball dropped gently through the net. The arena felt as if it were frozen in time as I made the move. As the ball went in, the crowd erupted. I found out later that one announcer on the television broadcast said at that moment, "And Eric Hanna just set St. John Arena on fire!" Penn State had no choice but to call time out. We had the lead and all the momentum in the world.

I was happy for the time out. At the moment, I was physically and emotionally spent. With all the events of the day, I was running on empty. Penn State would battle back, but we were still hanging on to a lead. Playing on borrowed time, I had one final highlight left in me. Titus Ivory drove down the middle of the lane. I was in good defensive help side position. He tried to jump stop at the end of his drive and avoid any contact, but he couldn't do it before he tapped my chest ever so slightly. I fell to the ground like I'd been run over by a pickup truck. The officials bought it. They called an offensive foul on him, giving us the ball back.

Neshaun Coleman was so pumped up, he came over and picked me up off the floor by the head. He practically ripped my ears off in the process as he shook me with pure elation. (That actually hurt much worse than the charge did.) The horn sounded for the under-eight-minute timeout, and Coach O'Brien subbed me out. This was a great decision, because I had nothing left. I needed a break. I felt exhausted, but very proud that I was able to contribute what I had.

All in all, I finished with nine points. Since then, I have often told people that Michael Redd and I combined for forty-one points that night. (Of course, Michael had thirty-two of them.) I had also stepped up on the defensive end of the floor, taking two charges. I think what I was most proud of, though, was that during the game, while I was on the court, we had won by thirteen points. In my mind, this meant that I ultimately gave our team a great chance to win. It was unfortunate for us that Penn State was able to finish off an overtime comeback, yet I couldn't help but feel good about giving everything I had in my last home game. I felt that those who came before me would have been proud of my efforts.

I could tell the fans appreciated our efforts as well. After the game was over, they packed the lower bowl area attempting to get the last game programs autographed. I gladly signed programs continuously for about forty-five minutes, and I would have kept going had it not been for friends and family pulling me out of the crowd.

HONORED

The last game in St. John Arena was the defining moment of my basketball career. It proved to me and others that an unconditional love for the game and an undying effort to become the best that you can be will translate into special memories regardless of how big your role is or how successful your team is. Another opportunity came in our final game of the season against Indiana in the first ever Big Ten Tournament and it reinforced my belief. While that contest was a 78–71 loss in the United Center in Chicago, I continued to be an integral part of our team, scrapping like crazy trying to turn our team's fortunes around. I didn't start that game, but I played nine minutes, scored another basket, and added a couple of rebounds, continuing to contribute as a regular in our line-up. My last collegiate highlight was battling forward

Luke Recker, Indiana Mr. Basketball 1997, for a loose ball. We both went after it with such fervor that the officials rushed over thinking we were fighting. We weren't fighting. We both just wanted to help our team win. This is the way I wanted to close things out. I was playing my best basketball at the end of my career and finishing up by leaving it all on the court. I was sending a message to our young players that if they work hard, good things would happen.

A few weeks later, I was a proud graduating senior at our annual basketball banquet. In lead up to the event, I recalled the banquet we had after my first stint on the team. I thought about the seniors and star players who won awards and received special league-wide honors. My second season ended with Coach Ayers being fired, and along with his exit went our banquet. This season, my senior season, I looked forward to our banquet to help me reflect on memories from a basketball career I cherished.

I was honored with the Fred Taylor Award, given to the player with the highest grade point average. I thanked my mother for all the support she had given me in my pursuits. I thanked my past and current coaches, including Coach Ayers, who gave me my first opportunity at Ohio State. I appreciated that my effort in the classroom had been recognized. I had worked hard to balance athletics and academics, and this award made me feel as if I had achieved that balance.

Not surprisingly, Michael Redd won the Jerry Lucas Most Valuable Player Award. Michael fought off double teams and gadget defenses throughout the year to lead the Big Ten in scoring as a freshman. A freshman had never led the league in scoring before. His future was bright, especially when Scoonie Penn was added to the back court the next season. I felt extremely honored to have had the opportunity to play with both of these special players.

Next was the John Havlicek Most Inspirational Player Award. When I heard my name called, a rush of emotion came over me. It had been a long journey from humble beginnings, including the many nights where I did not get off the bench during my high school years. In college, I took an even longer winding path of not playing, getting cut, making the team again, being awarded a scholarship and finally earning my way into the Buckeye lineup.

I couldn't help but think specifically of the year I had been cut and was working at Walt Disney World. I had purchased the autographed picture of John Havlicek, not only because I admired him so much as a player, but also to remember the special experience that helped me grow as a person. Now my name would always be associated with his in connection to this award. Moreover, it was very rewarding to think that my coaches felt I was a player who brought out the best in others. This award cemented in my mind that I belonged and contributed as a player at one of the finest athletic institutions in the country.

When I walked up to the podium to say thank you for the Havlicek Award, I was extremely humbled. I talked not only about what an honor the award was, but what a privilege it was to play for The Ohio State University. I never forgot how lucky I was to have had the opportunity to be a part of such a special experience.

Finally, Coach O'Brien talked about the season and the seniors. In his speech, he said, "There is no better compliment I can give Eric Hanna than to say he was a good teammate." At the time, I am not sure I valued this as much as I would later on in life. Looking back, I realize our treatment of others is more important than anything. No award I could receive could mean more than that type of praise from my coach. It really put my career journey into perspective. I always sought basketball glory. I set out on a path looking for it, thinking I would find it by starting on teams, scoring points, and winning big games. I found it when I realized it was more valuable to love being part of something bigger than yourself and to love the game itself. And at the end of the day, what more could I want in any walk of life?

CHAPTER 10
Fight to the End

A few months later, as I walked through Ohio Stadium to receive my diploma at the spring commencement ceremony, I was one of many students moving on from my college years to the next phase of life. Receiving diplomas with me that day were about ten thousand other enthusiastic graduates. A seventy-eight-page commencement book listed them all. Everyone at the ceremony was looking for a way to be seen through the masses by their family. Many students painted on their mortar boards, held signs, or carried balloons. I brought a basketball. I shot it up in the air from time to time so my mother could see where I was. I always felt like I had earned a separate degree in basketball, so this was a fitting way to close my collegiate career.

I set out to use my degree in business and interviewed for a variety of logistics and operations positions. One of the interviews was with a duct tape manufacturer in Avon, Ohio. When the interviewer asked where I saw myself down the road, I was honest. I told him I would love to be like Dean Smith. His poise and care for his players was legendary. Not surprisingly, with a response like this, I didn't get the job. They weren't looking to hire basketball coaches. I had another interview in Reynoldsburg, Ohio, for an operations management position. After giving similar answers, I was passed over again. This was definitely a sign that my heart was not in business. I decided I had to find a way to stay involved in basketball.

The athletics department offered me the opportunity to go back to Ohio State as a graduate assistant in Student Athlete Support Services. The position had me working with incoming student athletes who were learning to balance athletics and academics as they transitioned from high school to the Big Ten. I could help mold students while I pursued a master's degree in sports management and gained coaching experience. Ohio State couldn't take on volunteer coaches, so I went to nearby Capital University to help their men's program while I mentored Ohio State student athletes.

This translated into a very busy schedule, but the work I did was very rewarding, so I enjoyed the experience. I saw myself in many of the students I mentored. They were trying to fit long days of practice that brought endless fatigue together with high-level academic challenges. I encouraged them to keep fighting and stay focused. As an assistant coach, I learned how to motivate players and build lasting relationships. I enjoyed making connections with recruits as well.

I spent two years finishing my masters and three years at Capital coaching the men's program as a part-time assistant prior to landing a full-time position as an assistant coach at Vassar College in Poughkeepsie, New York. I moved there with high hopes of growing my coaching career. A month into my coaching tenure, America took an unexpected turn. On September 11, 2001, many people's lives were changed forever. Mine was as well, but in an unexpected way. While I was fortunate not to lose family members, and I wasn't actually in New York City during the catastrophic event, I watched the horrors from an hour away on television like many other Americans across the country. I had the same thoughts and feelings of sorrow, hurt, and anger that many Americans felt. My changes came from the soul-searching I did in the months following that tragic day.

During that time, I began to dig deep and think about what really mattered to me in life. I still loved basketball, so coaching was still a tremendous fit for me. But I was having trouble getting out of bed each day. I thought to myself, *What is missing? What would get me up and going every day even in a world full of question marks and doubt?* Finally, after much soul searching, I had an answer.

I had been blessed to have an amazing academic and athletic experience. So many positive role models inspired me to keep going along the way. I wanted the opportunity to help motivate others to achieve their dreams. I found solace in the idea that I could change young peoples' lives for the better.

I looked back at the times when I was in middle school and how desperately I needed coaches and teachers to inspire me each day. My entire journey finally made sense. I knew what I had to do. Before I even started my first full-time college coaching experience at Vassar, I applied for the Middle Childhood Education Program at Ohio State. My full-time college coaching career was over before it had started. I had found my calling. While I still very much wanted to be a coach, I had found what I needed to feel complete. I was going to be a teacher.

As a teacher and coach, I have two priorities that extend beyond any curriculum I am required to teach. First, I want my students to feel valued. After all, isn't this what everyone wants in life? Second, I want to motivate students to love learning and work hard at it so they can choose what they want to do in life instead of letting life choose for them. In my opinion, when the alarm clock goes off each day, we all want to be excited about where we are going and what we are doing. As a teacher and a coach, I always have this feeling.

Where does basketball fit into the picture? It is at the core of who I am. I consistently describe myself as a basketball addict. I always have been, and I always will be. I enjoy working with the player who barely made the squad and is trying to find a way to contribute as well as the star player who has huge pressure every night to help the team win. I relish the opportunity to help every player grow their love for the game.

To me, the game is a symphony of strategy. I look forward to working on late game situations and having the chance to draw up a play to win the game. I enjoy creating drills at practices that help players grow individually and collectively. At times, I still seek out the empty gym so I can shoot by myself and think through whatever is on my mind. I believe many of America's problems could be solved while shooting free throws or playing one-on-one in the driveway.

In the end, basketball will always be a part of who I am. The passion produced by those who love the game is so contagious and uplifting, it inspires me any time I see it. The game has taught me life lessons that I take with me everywhere I go. It can help anyone work through social differences and racial barriers. For me, basketball parallels life.

Along my basketball journey, I found the true value of the game. Initially, I let scoring, starting games, and winning drive my basketball experience. In the end, I found much more fulfilling reasons to play. The relationships, the competition, and the originality that came with every game and every team made each experience unique and rewarding.

I found that what I was really playing for was for the chance to be a part of something bigger than myself. When you love something so deeply and unconditionally, it is easy to fight to the end.

Ohio State vs. Penn State, February 28, 1998. Punctuating a Buckeye scoring run, Eric Hanna (44) finishes off a reverse lay-up during the second half of the last regular season game in the storied forty-two-year history of St. John Arena.

#44 Eric Hanna as a twenty-two-year-old senior at The Ohio State University. In his third year of playing for the Buckeyes, Eric finished as a three-time OSU Scholar Athlete, a two-time Academic All-Big Ten selection, and recipient of the 1998 Fred Taylor Award, and the 1998 John Havlicek Award.

It's "Eric Hanna Day" at College Traditions, a local Buckeye merchandise and apparel store on The Ohio State University campus in Columbus, Ohio. College Traditions frequently posted athlete's names for a day to show appreciation for their efforts throughout the season.

ABOUT THE AUTHOR
Eric Hanna

Born in Youngstown, Ohio, Eric Hanna was a walk-on basketball player for The Ohio State University from 1994–95 and 1996–98. During his senior season, his expertise on and off the court earned him a much sought-after basketball scholarship. He is a two-time Academic All-Big Ten selection (1997–98), a Fred Taylor Award Winner (1998), and a John Havlicek Award Winner (1998). Eric currently teaches American history at Shanahan Middle School in the Olentangy local school district where he earned the Battelle for Kids Celebrate Teaching Distinguished Educator Award in 2013. Eric has been an assistant basketball coach at Capital University (1998–2001, 2002–09), and at Vassar College (2001–02). Currently the youth basketball director for the Plain City Area Ball Association, Eric has coached basketball at every level, from kindergarten to college, since graduating from OSU.

CPSIA information can be obtained
at www.ICGtesting.com
Printed in the USA
FSHW011600130419
57230FS